The Legend of Inara Wali

OrangeBooks Publication

1st Floor, Rajhans Arcade, Mall Road, Kohka, Bhilai, Chhattisgarh 490020

Website: **www.orangebooks.in**

© Copyright, 2024, Author

All rights reserved. No part of this book may be reproduced, stored in a retrieval system, or transmitted, in any form by any means, electronic, mechanical, magnetic, optical, chemical, manual, photocopying, recording or otherwise, without the prior written consent of its writer.

First Edition, 2024

ISBN: 978-93-5621-420-0

THE LEGEND OF INARA WALI

PRASHANT KUMAR LAL

OrangeBooks Publication
www.orangebooks.in

To

Agastya, Pushpa,

Akash & Agnes

Books by the Same Author

- Science Unfolded for Std VI
- Science Unfolded for Std VII
- Science Unfolded for Std VIII
- Physics Test Series for class XII
- Image of my Experiences: A book of English Poetry
- Speeches from the Desk of the Principal
- The Legend of Inara Wali

Acknowledgement

The journey of bringing "The Legend of Inara Wali" to life has been one marked by perseverance, dedication, and unwavering support. This book, born from a short story penned in 1998, has traversed a long path, often lying forgotten under layers of dust and nearly lost to time. Yet, its resurrection into the form you hold today is a testament to the collective effort and passion of those dear to me.

Firstly, I owe an immense debt of gratitude to my wife, Agnes. A successful English teacher and accomplished author in her own right, Agnes has been my steadfast pillar of strength and inspiration. Her keen literary insight and unyielding encouragement breathed new life into this manuscript. She has been my most rigorous critic and my most ardent supporter, helping to shape and refine the narrative with her unparalleled expertise.

To my son, Advocate Akash Lal Joseph, I extend heartfelt thanks. His persistent persuasion to transform the original short story into a novel pushed me beyond my comfort zones. Our numerous discussions, debates, and sometimes spirited arguments were vital in honing the story's depth and direction. Akash's legal acumen and analytical mind provided fresh perspectives that were invaluable in crafting this book.

The process of writing, researching, and concluding this novel was an exhaustive endeavour that spanned many months, days, and nights. It was a labour of love that required not only intellectual rigor but also emotional resilience. Agnes and Akash not only contributed their insights but also provided me with the strength and amenities necessary to see this project through to its fruition. Their unwavering support and sacrifices are deeply appreciated.

I would also like to express my sincere appreciation to OrangeBooks Publication and its dedicated team. Your kindness and respect in receiving my work have made this journey less daunting and infinitely more rewarding. Your professionalism and commitment to excellence have been instrumental in bringing "The Legend of Inara Wali" to the readers.

Lastly, to you, dear reader, thank you for embarking on this journey with me. This book, close to my heart, is now ready to be shared, and I hope it resonates with you as deeply as it has with those who helped bring it to life.

With Heartfelt Gratitude,
Prashant Kumar Lal
Author

Preface

In the grand tapestry of human history, there exist certain individuals whose lives transcend the bounds of ordinary existence, leaving an indelible mark upon the collective consciousness of humanity. Among these luminaries stands Inara Wali, a figure whose name has become synonymous with the pursuit of justice, equality, and human dignity. In the pages of this book, titled " The Legend of Inara Wali" we embark on a journey through the corridors of time, exploring the remarkable legacy of a woman whose life serves as a testament to the enduring power of compassion and courage.

Through the lens of philosophical reflection and poetic expression, we delve into the heart of Sujata CDO's transformative journey, tracing her evolution from a humble advocate to a celebrated champion of social change. Each chapter unfolds with the lyrical grace of a timeless epic, inviting readers to immerse themselves in the rich tapestry of Sujata's experiences and insights.

As we navigate the labyrinthine passages of Sujata's life, we are confronted with profound questions of justice, equality, and the human condition. Through her unwavering dedication and tireless advocacy, Sujata challenges us to confront the systemic injustices that plague our society and to strive for a world where every individual is afforded the opportunity to flourish and thrive.

But "The Legend of Inara Wali" is more than a mere biography—it is a call to action, a rallying cry for all who aspire to make a difference in the world. Sujata's life serves as a powerful reminder that each of us has the capacity to effect change, to challenge the status quo, and to create a more just and equitable society for future generations.

As we embark on this literary odyssey, may we be inspired by Sujata's unwavering commitment to justice and equality. May her story ignite within us the flames of hope and resilience, and may we emerge from these pages with a renewed sense of purpose and determination to build a world where the ideals of justice, equality, and human dignity reign supreme.

With each turn of the page, may we honour the legacy of Inara Wali, and may her legend continue to inspire generations to come.

Prashant Kumar Lal
Author

About The Book

In the sacred annals of societal evolution, there exists a tome of profound significance—a testament to the transformative power of human endeavour and the enduring spirit of resilience and compassion. This book, a luminous beacon amidst the shadows of adversity, chronicles the remarkable journey of Sujata CDO, a luminary whose name has become synonymous with the principles of education, justice, equal opportunity, and human dignity.

Within its pages, the narrative unfolds with the lyrical cadence of a timeless epic, weaving together the threads of Sujata's unwavering dedication and tireless advocacy. Through the prism of her experiences, we are invited to traverse the landscape of social change, to witness the indomitable spirit of humanity in its quest for enlightenment and liberation.

At its core, this book is a philosophical treatise—a profound meditation on the nature of leadership, justice, and the inherent worth of every individual. Through Sujata's journey, we are reminded that true greatness lies not in the pursuit of personal glory, but in the service of others; not in the accumulation of wealth or power, but in the upliftment of the marginalized and the oppressed.

As we turn the pages, we are enveloped in a tapestry of wisdom and insight, each word a resplendent gem illuminating the path toward a more just and equitable society. From the hallowed halls of education to the corridors of justice, Sujata's influence reverberates, inspiring all who encounter her story to strive for a world where opportunity knows no bounds and dignity is the birthright of all.

But this book is more than a mere chronicle of events—it is a call to action, a clarion call to each of us to rise to our highest potential and become agents of change in our own right. For in the words of Sujata herself, "True progress is not measured by the heights we reach, but by the depth of our compassion and the breadth of our empathy."

In honouring Sujata and her extraordinary legacy, we honour the very essence of our shared humanity—the belief that each of us, regardless of our background or circumstance, has the power to make a difference in the world. May this book serve as a testament to the enduring power of hope, the resilience of the human spirit, and the transformative potential of love and solidarity.

In the realm of literature, this journey finds its echo in the stories we tell, the tales we weave with words. As an author, I am but a humble bard, seeking to capture the essence of this journey in the pages of my works. Through prose and poetry, I strive to shine a light on the triumphs and tribulations of those who dare to defy the odds, who dare to dream of a world where education knows no boundaries.

For in the end, it is not the accolades or the acclaim that define our success as authors, but rather the impact we leave on the hearts and minds of those who read our words. And if, in some small measure, my writings can inspire even a single soul to embrace the transformative power of education, then I shall consider my pen truly blessed.

Content

1. Malanga 1
2. Inara: Life's Simple Melodies 6
3. Rudra and Kusum 11
4. Sorrowful Widow's Solitary Existence 17
5. Widow's Plight: Ancient Tragedies 25
6. Mahendra Park 31
7. Affluent's Opposition Unfolds 46
8. Rise of Inara Wali 52
9. Towns' Talk – Hope Awakens 61
10. Open Sky School Success 70
11. She was Twenty – Five 79
12. Mahesh & Inara Wali 83
13. Shrimati Geeta Devi High School – A Royal Decree 86
14. Social Justice Conversation At The Panchayat Library .. 94
15. Library Battle: Equality Defended 106
16. Love's Eternal Melody 111
17. Community Voice Rises 116
18. Unity Vs Division 125

19. A Big Operation Unfolds 137

20. Passionate Love Blossoms 153

21. Unseen Chains: Ideological Battle 166

22. Prison Power Dynamics 180

23. Elder's Retaliation and Consequences 187

24. First Civil Service Success 197

25. "Echoes Of Change: The Transformative Journey Of Sujata And Mahesh" 211

26. A Weekend Of Reflections And Resolutions 216

27. Village Evolutionary Shift 222

28. Nandini & Suman: Their Plight And Influence 228

29. The Escape of Bhola Singh 242

30. The Decision Of Heart And Mind 257

31. Family Reunion 275

32. Bhola Singh's Conspiracy 286

33. Finale of the Legend 295

1

Malanga

Amidst the sprawling plains of Madhesh Province in Nepal, nestled a town of profound history and rich cultural tapestry – Malanga. This enclave, steeped in tradition and brimming with the echoes of time, stood as the venerable heart of Sarlai District. Its origins whispered tales of antiquity, woven into the very fabric of its existence. Malanga, ensconced in the embrace of the Mahendra Highway, adorned the landscape like a jewel, beckoning travellers with its allure. A town steeped in reverence, it owed its name to the legendary Malang Baba, a revered saint whose spirit lingered in the hearts of both Hindus and others alike. Each year, the town adorned itself in festivity, paying homage to this revered figure amidst the vibrant hues of Chaitra.

Beneath the azure skies, Malanga blossomed, its population a mosaic of diverse backgrounds – from the steadfast Madhesis to the vibrant Newaris and Marwadis. Here, amidst the verdant embrace of nature, life unfolded in a rhythm as old as time itself. Yet, beyond the veneer of tranquillity lay a land fraught with challenges. The capricious monsoons, wielding their tempestuous might, dictated the ebb and flow of life, bestowing bounty upon the land yet also veiling it in the cloak of uncertainty. The Terai, once a formidable barrier, now stood as a testament to resilience, its marshes and forests guarding the land against the spectre of invasion.

But amidst the trials, Malanga thrived, a testament to the indomitable spirit of its people. From the bustling markets to the tranquil temples, each corner whispered tales of resilience and fortitude. The echoes of its past, though tinged with strife, resonated with a quiet dignity, a reminder of the town's enduring legacy. In the realm of culture, Malanga stood as a bastion of tradition, its air infused with the melodies of community radio stations and the rustle of newspapers. Here, amidst the modern cacophony, the spirit of heritage thrived, weaving a tapestry of stories that transcended time itself.

And yet, amidst the tapestry of life, shadows lurked in the corners. From the echoes of past conflicts to the spectre of modern-day challenges, Malanga stood as a crucible of resilience, its spirit unyielding in the face of adversity. But amidst the trials, a beacon of hope shone brightly - the spirit of Sujata, a woman of resolute courage and unwavering resolve. In her, the town found its champion, a symbol of defiance against the shackles of tradition and the prejudices of society.

As the sun dipped below the horizon, casting its golden glow upon the town, Malanga stood as a testament to the enduring spirit of humanity. For here, amidst the trials and tribulations of life, hope blossomed like a lotus in the murky waters of adversity, illuminating the path to a brighter tomorrow. In the quaint village of Malanga, nestled on the edge of India, a narrative of resurgence unfurled nearly four decades ago. Adjacent lay Chandbarsha, a settlement entrenched within Indian boundaries, separated from Malanga by the confluence of the Nepalese river, JHEEM. Amidst this junction stood a venerable peepal tree, its roots intertwined with the annals of time. Though its branches were sparse, a singular V-shaped bough bore the emblem of triumph. It was beneath this arboreal sentinel, known locally as Puttali Gacch that Nepalese law enforcement diligently patrolled. As the inaugural rays of dawn caressed Malanga, they filtered through the branches of Puttali Gacch, ushering in a new day laden with destiny and determination, never straying towards Chandbarsha, for Malanga lay westward in this remote domain.

This segment of the Indo-Nepal border languished in obscurity, devoid of significant commercial activity. It lacked the necessary infrastructure for smuggling operations, be it narcotics or firearms. The local populace, inherently pragmatic, eschewed involvement in illicit trades. Instead, the residents of Malanga resorted to selling their wares in the weekly market at Chandbarsha under the guise of bootlegging. Amidst these clandestine exchanges, Puttali Gacch stood sentinel, witnessing the transactions unfold. Farmers tallied their earnings, thieves divided their spoils, and even law enforcement officers assessed their gains, all beneath the watchful gaze of Puttali Gacch. Yet, despite its keen observations, the ancient tree seemed burdened by the weight of its own wisdom, perpetually perplexed by the multitude of sights and experiences it bore witness to.

In the heartland of Nepal's Sarlai district, the picturesque town of Malanga unfolds like a drapery woven with threads of distinct heritage. Settled amidst the fertile lands, its inhabitants trace their origins to the cradle of India, their essence reminiscent of the vibrant hues of Bihar. Within its bounds, a melange of cultures converges in harmonious symphony, casting an illusion of Indianness upon its facade. Amidst the labyrinth of winding streets, a handful of natives find solace alongside the Madhesees, denizens of the terai region. Here, the Madhesees reign supreme, a mosaic of Muslims, schedule castes, and the esteemed upper echelons of society. Yet, amidst this societal tapestry, a bittersweet truth lingers—a dichotomy of recognition. Many castes, relegated to the margins, are branded with the labels signifying the burden of status complexities in this intricate societal fabric.

Nestled at the twilight edge of Malanga, where the whispers of its streets blend seamlessly with the distant echoes of Indian territory, stood an arboreal titan: the revered 'Puttali Gachh.' Beneath its sprawling canopy, time itself seemed to slow, as if enraptured by the tales whispered among its ancient leaves. This majestic Peepal tree, an emblem of continuity and resilience, bore witness to the ebb and flow of joy and despair, assuming the mantle of a celestial sentinel in the lives of those it sheltered. With each rustle of its verdant foliage, it wove stories, becoming a silent confidant to the secrets of the human heart. In the delicate dance of light and shadow beneath its boughs, one could discern the sacred bond between earth and sky, and feel the gentle embrace of nature's enduring grace. Truly, the 'Puttali Gachh' stood as a monument to the enduring spirit of hope and guardianship, a lighthouse of solace amidst the ever-shifting currents of existence.

The Legend of Inara Wali

2

Inara: Life's Simple Melodies

In the gentle embrace of the Janaknandini rural council, nestled within the verdant embrace of Dhanushka District in the heart of south-eastern Nepal, lies the quaint hamlet of Inara. Here, time seems to slow to the rhythm of the land, where the whispering winds carry tales of generations past and present.

Ward no. 1 of Janaknandini rural council cradles Inara, a village that boasts a rich theme of history and community spirit. Like a precious gem adorning the landscape, Inara reveals its population of few thousand souls, each a vibrant thread in the knotty frame of village life.

In the symphony of governance, Inara dances to the tune of the village development committee, a cornerstone of local administration in the Nepalese countryside. Within its boundaries, the village development committee orchestrates a harmonious partnership between the community and the public sector, weaving together dreams of progress and prosperity.

Under the benevolent gaze of elected chiefs and dedicated ward members, Inara thrives as an autonomous institution, empowered to shape its own destiny. From education to sanitation, from water supply to income generation, the village development committee stands as a guardian of the collective welfare, ensuring the equitable distribution of resources and the meticulous recording of progress.

Yet, like a river flowing ever forward, change sweeps across the tranquil landscape of Inara. Few years ago, the village development committee structure yielded to the dawn of a new era, making way for the advent of village-palika. A transformation heralded by the constitution of Nepal in 1990, it reshapes the contours of governance, merging old boundaries and forging new paths towards a brighter future.

As the pages of history turn, Inara remains a testament to the enduring spirit of community and resilience, where the past meets the present, and the promise of tomorrow shimmers on the horizon like an ideal of hope.

Half a century ago, the quaint hamlet of Inara lay nuzzled amidst rolling hills, its population sparse and intimate, numbering only a few hundred souls. Here, amidst the verdant embrace of nature, there existed no formal organization, no guiding hand to weave the fabric of town planning or orchestrate the symphony of communal welfare. Instead, the rhythms of life danced to the ancient melodies of tradition, where each day unfolded with the simplicity of ages past.

Inara's landscape was adorned with humble dwellings, not of concrete majesty, but fashioned from the very earth itself, where walls of mud whispered tales of cohorts. Within these rustic abodes, families dwelled in harmony, bound by the sacred ties of kinship, sharing both joys and sorrows beneath the sheltering cuddle of communal unity.

Life unfurled with the rhythm of seasons, and sustenance was drawn from the generous bosom of the land. Men toiled in the fields, their attire simple yet dignified, clad in loin cloth that bore witness to the toil of labour, while a thin towel draped around their necks served as a testament to their resilience against the sun's relentless gaze.

Women, adorned in the elegance of simplicity, adorned themselves in sarees sans blouse, their grace transcending the confines of modesty, as the innocence of youth found solace beneath layers of translucent fabric, veiling the allure of femininity with a delicate modesty.

In the midst of the fields and pastures, the air was alive with the lilting melodies of labour, as men and women alike lent their voices to the chorus of nature's symphony. Their songs, woven with the threads of native tongue, celebrated the beauty of the land, the allure of love, and the timeless pleasures of existence, echoing across the verdant expanse in harmonious resonance.

In the restful cuddle of twilight, the village stirred with life's complex dance. Men, their silhouettes etched against the fading light, congregated in intimate clusters, their laughter mingling with the whispers of the evening breeze. Meanwhile, the women, embodiments of grace and resilience, bent over hearths and looms, weaving the fabric of familial warmth.

In the heart of Inara, where the rhythm of life frolicked to the gentle flicker of lanterns and the warm glow of kerosene lamps, darkness held court each evening, casting the village streets in a cloak of obsidian velvet. Yet, amidst the shadows, a celestial symphony unfolded above, painting the heavens with a canvas of inky depth, each star a luminary jewel in the areas of the night.

In this ambit untouched by the electric hum of modernity, time itself was measured not by the tick of a clock, but by the graceful ascent and descent of celestial sentinels, revered as ancient guardians of the village's temporal curtains. With a profound reverence and intimate understanding, the villagers sought solace and guidance in the celestial ballet, finding in its silent cadence a timeless connection to the cosmos. Amidst this bustling tableau, children wove through the gathering, their laughter a symphony of youthful exuberance. Like playful sprites, they chased one another with abandon, their laughter echoing through the village square. As the men indulged in the nectar of camaraderie, savouring the earthy tang of locally brewed wine, the night unfurled its mysteries. Yet, within this stuff of revelry, shadows lurked. For some, the intoxicating brew unleashed untamed passions, transforming laughter into tumult, as primal urges surged unchecked.

In the hushed corners of their homes, some men returned bearing the weight of their masculinity like a tempest, their voices thundering against walls, their hands wielding echoes of anguish. Yet, amidst the discord, others returned with hearts brimming with tenderness, their love an example amidst the storm. Amidst the tumult, the elders, venerable custodians of tradition, cradled the next generation in the embrace of storytelling. Beneath the canopy of stars, they wove tales of yore, their voices a balm to young souls, amidst the discord or the whispered caresses of moonlit passion.

With the dawn, a new chapter unfolded, bathed in the golden hues of sunrise. Each morning heralded fresh aspirations, each sunrise painting anew the canvas of their lives. Amidst the ebb and flow of routine, amidst the familiar embrace of kinship, the village danced to the rhythm of life's eternal cadence.

3

Rudra and Kusum

In the heart of Inara nestled a humble abode - where resided Rudra and his beloved wife, Kusum. Rudra, a figure of imposing stature, possessed a commanding presence, his dark complexion and piercing gaze striking fear into the hearts of those who crossed his path. Yet, beneath this formidable exterior lay a man of great strength and resilience, known throughout the village as the indomitable force of Inara.

His days were spent in the solemn duty of tending to the departed creatures of the land. With hands weathered by toil and marked by the stains of blood and fat, Rudra undertook the solemn task of disposing of the deceased livestock, ensuring that the sanctity of the village remained undisturbed. His livelihood intertwined with the cycle of life and death, as he skilfully transformed animal hides into sought-after commodities, sustaining his family through the fruits of his labour.

Weekends brought forth a different rhythm to Rudra's existence, as he emerged from the shadows of his daily routine to ply his trade in the bustling marketplace. There, amidst the aroma of freshly caught fish and the savory scent of mutton, Rudra would offer his wares to the eager villagers, his hands adept at the art of commerce despite their roughened exterior.

Yet, despite his indispensable role in the fabric of village life, Rudra remained an outcast in the eyes of many. The remnants of his labour clung to his being, casting him as an untouchable figure in the eyes of society. Shunned from the sacred halls of the village temple and relegated to the fringes of communal life, Rudra and his family existed on the margins, their presence a reminder of the fragility of societal norms.

Far removed from the heart of the village, Rudra's dwelling stood as a testament to his isolation, a simple thatched roof sheltering his beloved wife, Kusum, and their five children from the world outside. Yet, within these humble confines, love and resilience flourished, binding the family together in the face of adversity.

Thus, amidst the dichotomy of acceptance and rejection, Rudra's life unfolded, a testament to the complexities of human existence and the enduring power of the human spirit to persevere against all odds.

In the quaint embrace of the village, Kusum, adorned in scanty attire, her hair entwined in wild tangles, and her visage untouched by the artifice of makeup, possessed an allure that stirred the hearts of men. Yet, this beguiling presence, akin to a delicate bloom amidst a rugged landscape, was a double-edged sword, drawing the gaze of envious eyes and igniting desires veiled behind superficial charm.

Alone, she treaded cautiously, her femininity a beacon for unwarranted advances and lecherous propositions. With each step to fetch water or procure provisions, she bore the weight of unwanted attention, the well's custodian offering his liquid bounty from a safe distance, while lascivious whispers and indecent proposals punctuated her every endeavour.

In silent resignation, she bore the burden of this clandestine struggle, concealing the indignities suffered beneath a veil of stoic resolve. Unable to confide in her husband, she navigated this labyrinth of disgraces with practiced poise, accepting castoff garments from sympathetic villagers and fending off advances with a subtle dance of flirtation, a defence mechanism born of necessity.

Yet, amidst the shadows of her tribulations, a glimmer of compassion flickered. For even in her own plight, she extended kindness, accepting men's advances with a coy smile, a gesture meant to soften the jagged edges of their desires. And in return, she was met with scorn and suspicion, the village women casting her as the temptress, a siren luring their husbands astray. Bound by the unspoken rules of village life, Rudra and Kusum found themselves relegated to the fringes, tasked with menial chores and offered the scraps of society's bounty. But beneath the weight of their station, a quiet resilience blossomed, a testament to the indomitable spirit that thrived amidst adversity.

In the quiet depths of Rudra's heart, a ceaseless worry took dwelling, a concern that intertwined with the very mess of his being - the upbringing of his five cherished children. His desire was singular yet profound: to bestow upon them the gift of equality, to pave their path with opportunities as vast and boundless as the horizon itself. Yet, despite his fervent aspirations, Rudra witnessed a poignant absence in their lives - the laughter of unrestrained joy remained but an elusive melody, the taste of culinary delights tailored to their palates a distant dream, and the clothes to clothe their frames a luxury beyond reach.

Immersed in the depths of his own helplessness, his weary form and tired mind sought solace in the clasp of slumber. It was then, amidst the realms of dreams, that Rudra's consciousness transcended the bounds of his reality, venturing into a realm where the ethereal danced with the tangible, and the mystical whispered secrets to the mortal soul.

In this surreal vision, a peculiar entity stood sentinel upon the banks of a river named Jheem, in a far-flung village known as Malanga, nestled snugly along the Indo-Nepal border. It was a peepal tree, but not just any - its branches stretched skyward, adorned with a canopy of verdant leaves that shimmered in the gentle caress of the wind. The air was alive with whispers, the branches swaying in a symphony orchestrated by the playful breeze that carried the essence of the nearby river's cool embrace.

In this sacred communion of nature, a name resonated through the ether, a name that bore the essence of Rudra's heart and soul - Sujata, his beloved daughter, the third jewel in his familial crown. As if beckoned by an unseen force, the spirit of Sujata danced upon the whispers of the wind, her presence felt in every rustle of the leaves, every ripple upon the tranquil surface of the river.

For Rudra, this dream was more than mere illusion - it was a revelation, an indication to the interconnectedness of all things, and a hope that illuminated the path toward a future where his children would know the joys of laughter unbounded, the flavours of culinary delight, and the warmth of clothing to adorn their forms. And as he lingered in the celestial vision, Rudra found solace, for in the whispers of the wind and the rustle of leaves, he found the promise of a brighter tomorrow, where equality reigned supreme and his children would flourish beneath the shade of the Puttali Gachh, in the village of Malanga, upon the banks of the river Jheem.

As Rudra stirred from slumber, the tendrils of sleep reluctantly releasing their grasp, he found himself ensnared in a warren of confusion. A dream, vivid and haunting, lingered like morning mist in his mind's eye. It was woven with threads of perplexity, where his third daughter danced in the forefront, her presence singular and enigmatic.

Beneath the cloak of sleep, his consciousness wrestled with the puzzle: why her, and why now? Why did she traverse the winding paths leading to Malanga, a place etched in the tapestry of his memories? And what curious connection lay veiled between Sujata and the Puttali Gachh, that sacred grove of whispered secrets and ancient wisdom?

Each question, a silent sentinel standing guard over the sphere of his thoughts, offered no succour, no immediate respite from the enigma that enveloped him. Yet, amid the tumult of uncertainty, a timid ember of relief flickered to life within him. In the quietude of dawn, Rudra found himself tangled in a web of wonder and bewilderment, his heart heavy with the weight of unanswered riddles, yet buoyed by the faint promise of understanding yet to unfold.

4

Sorrowful Widow's Solitary Existence

In the whispering halls of time, the destiny unfurled, revealing the profound and eternal ripples of those deemed 'status complexities'. Puttali Gacch, with its bald visage and sardonic gaze, stood as a picket of truth, unwavering in its resolve. It refused to falter in the face of misfortune, for it bore the weight of countless journeys yet to unfold, traversing endless miles upon miles of existence's boundless expanse.

In the distant reaches of Malanga, a Nepalese town secluded from the bustling currents of modern education, a single blaze of learning flickered faintly—a modest middle school overseen by the venerable Marwari figure, Shri Ardas Mal Bajaj. Here, amidst the hushed tales of convention and the weighty veils that shrouded the womenfolk, a silent dance of roles played out.

Within the confines of their veils, women dwelled, their voices but echoes in the shadows, veiled not just by cloth, but by the veils of tradition and societal expectation. Communication with their husbands was a twirl of whispers, confined to the shadows of the day, their covers - a constant reminder of their place in this stagnant tableau.

In the rigid hierarchies of Malanga, where 'gharwalas' and 'gharwalis' moved in silent tandem, life lingered, caught in the endless loop of tradition and expectation. Yet, amidst the stillness, a subtle shift began to stir—a quiet rebellion born of necessity and longing. It was the women, with their silent strength and resilient spirit, who dared to defy the suffocating labels imposed upon them. No longer content to be mere appendages to their husbands' names, they sought out new identities, names that spoke of their origins, their lineage, their essence. Thus, from the suffocating confines of 'gharwalis', they emerged as radiant beings, bearing the names of their ancestral homes—Sundarpur Wali, Brahampur Wali, Ratanpur Wali, and countless others. In reclaiming their identities, they forged new paths, reshaping the very brickwork of Malanga's society with each whispered declaration of self. For in the heart of every 'Wali' beat the pulse of rebellion, the quiet insistence that they were more than just shadows in the Malanga's existence. They were the architects of their own destinies, the bearers of light in a world shrouded in darkness, and in their names, a new chapter of defiance and dignity unfolded, casting a radiant glow upon the silent streets of Malanga.

In the mists of time preceding the era of Rana's ascendancy in the heartlands of Nepal, there emerged a figure of ethereal grace near the tranquil expanse of Puttali Gacch. Hers was a tale woven with threads of sorrow and innocence, for Sujata was wedded to a mere child of eight, only to be cruelly bereaved by fate's unforgiving hand soon thereafter. Amid the shadows of grief, she remained untethered to the memory of her brief union. A mere tender sapling of five winters when betrothed, her ancestral roots dug deep in the soil of Inara, casting her identity forever as the enchanting "Inara Wali," a name whispered with reverence and mystery upon the lips of those who dared to tread the paths of antiquity.

In the tranquil clasp of nature, Puttali Gacch, with its ancient roots firmly grounded, held within its silent wisdom the tincture of all that surrounded it. Each sigh of the breeze and every placid sway of its branches spoke volumes to the keen observer, revealing not only the intricacy of the world but also the unspoken desires and destinies of those who sought solace beneath its leafy canopy. With a wisdom transcending language, it deciphered the subtle nuances etched upon the brows of passersby, discerning the pathways they were fated to tread. Though mute in human tongue, this venerable tree remained a stoic witness to the joys and sorrows of life, silently grieving for the unacknowledged burdens carried by those who wandered its shadowed realm.

In the antiquated hamlet of Malanga, there dwelled a woman of enigmatic allure, known to many as Inara Wali, yet her true name whispered in the winds of forgotten tales was Sujata. Her presence stirred whispers amongst the cobblestone paths, for few knew of the drapery of her past.

In the pretty town of Malanga, settled amidst rolling hills and verdant landscapes, there existed a tale of youthful innocence intertwined with the solemnity of tradition. Here, under the gentle caress of the sun's golden rays, two souls, Rudra and Kusum, toiled tirelessly to forge a path for their beloved daughter.

Their efforts bore fruit as they orchestrated the union of their cherished six-year-old daughter with a boy of eight, a union bound by the threads of tradition and familial honour. Amid the joyous celebrations and fragrant blossoms adorning the village square, a poignant truth lingered beneath the surface.

For Rudra, with his weathered hands and eyes that gleamed with a quiet fervour, saw in this union not just a solemn ritual but a hope, a testament to his firm belief in a sunnier future. His gaze, imbued with dreams and aspirations, illuminated the path ahead, guiding his family through the life's intricacies.

However, as the laughter of children swayed upon the calm breeze, it became evident that innocence reigned utmost in the hearts of the young bride and groom. Oblivious to the weight of tradition and the solemn vows exchanged in their name, they frolicked in the ephemeral embrace of childhood, their minds untethered by the complexities of adulthood.

In the midst of this juxtaposition of tradition and innocence, the essence of childhood gripped, casting a nostalgic hue over the proceedings. For in the eyes of Rudra and Kusum, as they beheld their children's laughter and playful antics, lay the timeless truth that amidst life's grand event, it is the simplicity of joy and the purity of love that truly endure.

In the tender bloom of her youth, Sujata found herself ensnared in the web of adulthood long before her time.

Entrusted to the care of her in-laws, she became a reluctant pupil in the school of matrimony, a curriculum far beyond her comprehension. Veiled in garments of modesty, her innocent visage shrouded, she navigated the labyrinthine corridors of duty and expectation.

With gentle hands, she stirred the cauldron of familial sustenance, her nimble fingers weaving tales of nourishment and obligation. Amidst the aromatic symphony of spices, the melody of her laughter remained but a distant echo, silenced by the weight of tradition. Forbidden were the joys of uninhibited play, her world confined to the domestic hearth, where the flickering flames whispered secrets of a life yet untasted.

Beneath the veil, her spirit yearned for the light of freedom, the embrace of carefree days spent in youthful abandon. Yet, like a fledgling denied the sky, she fluttered within the confines of expectation, her wings clipped by the hands of conformity. Thus, in the silent chambers of her heart, the melody of childhood remained unsung, a poignant refrain lost amidst the clamour of societal dictates. In the tranquil expanse beyond the village's edge, nestled within the embrace of rolling hills, dwelled the in-laws of Sujata. Their homestead hummed with the industrious rhythm of life intertwined with nature's cycles. Amidst the thriving backdrop, they diligently tended to the solemn task of handling the remains of creatures departed, skilfully transforming them into sustenance for their community.

Each week, as the sun cast its golden rays upon the bustling market square, they would unveil their offerings of meat and fish, an evidence to their labour and the bounty of the land. This bustling commerce, unfurled a silent journey.

Across distant paths, the women of the household boarded on a pilgrimage to the well of Mukhiya ji, the venerable village headman. Their journey, impermeable to perseverance, led them to the lifeblood of their experience - water.

In this choreographed ballet of existence, even the mundane rituals bore the mark of tradition and duty. Mukhiya Ji's appointed custodian, positioned at a distance, carefully poured forth the elixir of life into their waiting vessels, bridging the gap between need and fulfilment.

In the symphony of daily life, Sujata found herself laced seamlessly into the fabric of tradition and expectation, her aspirations tethered to the timeless prototypes of her familial legacy. In Malanga, as in her ancestral home, the existence unfolded with familiar grace, etching her journey into the annals of tradition and continuity.

In the heart of her community, Sujata stood as a singular grace and wisdom, distinct from her peers in both demeanour and perception. Her soul, tuned to the delicate human interaction, possessed a rare gift—a profound ability to unravel the enigma of circumstance and character alike.

With each passing day, she wove the threads of her existence into growth and self-discovery, her spirit striving ever skyward, yearning to ascend beyond the confines of expectation. Through the gentle passage of time, she gleaned the essence of life's essential teachings, mastering the subtle dance of existence with a poise beyond her years.

As the petals of her youth unfurled, so too did her understanding of the world around her, blossoming into a profound awareness that eclipsed the innocence of her tender years. In the tender clinch of maturation, she found herself traversing landscapes of societal nuance with a clarity that eluded even those of more advanced age, her insights illuminating the path ahead with an incandescent brilliance that belied her tender years.

In the tender bloom of her fourteenth year, Sujata was swiftly swept into the cruel embrace of fate's caprice. The man whom she had wed, her ideal of dream and love, succumbed to the relentless grasp of an incurable malady, leaving her to navigate the treacherous seas of widowhood at an age when most souls are yet sheltered in the warmth of youthful dreams. A torrent of anguish besieged her fragile heart, each passing moment a symphony of grief echoing through the chambers of her soul. Clad in the sombre garb of mourning, she stood as a spectre of sorrow, her once vibrant spirit shrouded in the pall of loss. Time, that relentless sculptor of destinies, etched its mark upon her being, shaping her existence into solitude and seclusion. Bound by the solemn rites dictated by tradition, she adorned herself in the purity of white, a symbol of her perpetual lamentation, while sustenance came in the form of humble fare, devoid of the spices that once ignited the flames of joy within her.

Laughter, that ephemeral melody of life, became but a distant memory, banished by the decree of societal diktat. In the shadowed confines of her existence, she lived as a ghost among the living, her presence a silent testament to the fragility of human fortune and the inexorable march of time's indifferent march. As the tragic tale of Sujata unfolded beneath its aging boughs, Puttali Gachh, once a verdant haven of life, underwent a sombre transformation. Each leaf, once a vibrant testament to vitality, now fell like tearful confessions, littering the ground in a silent lament. The very essence of spring seemed to wither in its embrace, as if the season itself dared not disturb the sorrow that cloaked the tree.

Where once throngs of people sought solace in its shade, a palpable void now lingered, drawing a respectful distance from the tree's melancholic aura. Even the laughter of children, once the symphony of playful innocence, fell silent, replaced by hushed whispers of caution and fear. It was as though Puttali Gachh, in a poignant display of solidarity, had woven itself into Sujata's mourning, its branches reaching out in silent empathy to the depths of her sorrow.

5

Widow's Plight: Ancient Tragedies

In ancient times, the plight of widows in Indo – Nepal sub- continent was a tragic testament to the depths of societal expectations and cultural traditions. Widows, particularly young girls thrust into widowhood, bore the weight of responsibilities far beyond their tender years. Forced to navigate the muddle of adulthood without the guidance of education or skills, they grappled with the burdens of earning a living, nurturing their offspring, and assuming roles of both mother and father.

Tragically, in some regions, widows were subjected to the harrowing practice of sati, where they were expected to immolate themselves on their husband's funeral pyre, a ghastly ritual steeped in tradition and perceived honour. The very notion of widowhood carried with it an aura of ill omen and societal ostracization, relegating these women to lives of seclusion and deprivation.

Amidst the darkness, there were flickers of reform and compassion. Visionaries like Ishwar Chandra Vidyasagar dared to challenge the status quo, advocating for the rights and dignity of widows. Their efforts paved the way for legislative changes, such as the Widow

Remarriage Act of 1856 in India, which offered a glimmer of hope amidst the shadows of tradition.

The resilience of widows, often depicted as Krishna's gopis, is a testament to the enduring spirit of human perseverance. Though faced with adversity and sorrow, they found solace in their faith and their unwavering commitment to life's journey, guided by the divine presence of Krishna himself. Theirs is a story of quiet strength and untold sacrifice, laced into the sub - continent's rich history and tradition.

Inara Wali, a name whispered through the corridors of time, embodied the kernel of strength amidst adversity. Widowed in her tender years, she found herself cast adrift in the tumultuous currents of fate, her innocence eclipsed by the shadows of grief and responsibility.

Malanga, a land steeped in tradition and teeming with whispers of bygone eras, became both the cradle and crucible of Inara Wali's journey. Here, amidst the verdant fields and rustling palms, she embarked on a pilgrimage of the soul, navigating the warren of her existence with grace and fortitude.

In the hushed whispers of Malanga's ancient streets, Inara Wali learned to dance to the rhythm of life's symphony, her feminine posture a testament to the delicate balance of strength and vulnerability. Like a lotus rising from murky waters, she epitomized the beauty that blossoms in adversity, her spirit untarnished by the trials of widowhood.

Amid the ebb and flow of life's tides, Inara Wali refused to be shackled by the chains of societal expectation. With each step she took, she defied the limitations imposed upon her gender, thirsting for knowledge like a parched desert yearns for rain. In the quiet corners of Malanga's libraries, she delved into the realms of wisdom and enlightenment, her mind a beacon of illumination in a world shrouded in darkness.

Education became her sanctuary, a sacred haven where she sought refuge from the unbridled currents of her survival. Through the pages of ancient texts and the muttered teachings of sages, she discovered the power of knowledge to transcend the boundaries of circumstance and shaped her destiny.

Yet, in the course of her pursuit of illumination, Inara Wali never lost sight of her social onuses. Like a silent guardian, she clasped the mantle of responsibility, knitting the threads of compassion and duty of her being. Though burdened with the weight of adulthood from a tender age, she bore her cross with dignity and grace, her heart a wellspring of compassion in a world fraught with suffering.

Inara Wali's journey, though beset with trials and tribulations, was a testament to the indomitable spirit of the human soul. Through her story, we are reminded of the transformative power of resilience, the enduring beauty of the human spirit, and the boundless potential that lies within each and every one of us.

Inara Wali, a solitary figure, bore the weight of her burdens with the grace of a wounded dove. As she ventured forth each day to graze the goats and cattle, she walked a tightrope between the innocence of childhood and the harsh realities of adulthood. Yet, even as the village boys hurled their taunts like arrows, she remained steadfast in her resolve, her spirit unyielding in the facade of inconvenience.

With each stride, she carried the weight of her family's sustenance upon her slender shoulders, her hands calloused from the toil of tending to their needs. Cooking over an open flame, she wove culinary magic from the humblest of ingredients, transforming scarcity into abundance with the alchemy of her love.

Despite the cacophony of her daily struggles, Inara Wali found solace in the quiet moments of her existence. Beneath the shade of an ancient peepal tree, she sought refuge from the harsh realities of her world, her fingers tracing the delicate contours of parchment as she unravelled the mysteries of letters and words.

In the wisdoms of her solitude, she forged a bond with the written word, a silent companion in a world fraught with noise and chaos. With each stroke of her quill, she etched her hopes and dreams upon the canvas of her imagination, her aspirations soaring like a kite caught in the winds of destiny.

Yet, even as she danced upon the precipice of poverty and want, Inara Wali remained undaunted in her quest for knowledge. With each page turned, she cast aside the shackles of ignorance, her thirst for learning a flame that burned bright amidst the darkness of her circumstances.

Inara Wali's journey, though fraught with hardship and adversity, is an authentication to the resilience of the human spirit. Through her trials and tribulations, she emerged as a hope in a world shrouded in despair, her unwavering grit a tribute to the transformative power of the human soul.

As the first rays of daylight patted the horizon, painting the sky in hues of rose and gold, the ancient peepal tree exuded an aura of serenity, its roots anchored deep within the earth, connecting past, present, and future in a sacred dance of life.

As Inara Wali, the solitary figure whose footsteps echoed through the quiet streets, began to emerge from the shadows of her grief, a subtle shift rippled through the fabric of the natural world. The leaves of Puttali Gachh, once sombre and still, now rustled with a newfound vitality, whispering secrets of hope and renewal to the breeze that twirled amongst its branches.

Each leaf seemed to tremble with anticipation, unfurling its delicate veins like fingers reaching for the sun. Bathed in the morning light, the canopy of Puttali Gachh swayed gently, a symphony of green and gold that echoed the joy radiating from Inara Wali's heart.

The birds, ever vigilant in their perch amidst the boughs, joined in the chorus of celebration, their melodious songs filling the air with a dissonance of jubilation. From the smallest sparrow to the mightiest eagle, every winged creature seemed to take flight, their feathers shimmering like jewels in the dappled sunlight.

Even the creatures of the forest, hidden from view amongst the undergrowth, seemed to sense the shift in the air. Squirrels chattered excitedly as they scampered from branch to branch, while rabbits emerged from their burrows to bask in the warmth of the morning sun. But perhaps most wondrous of all was the transformation that swept through the very heart of Puttali Gachh itself. As Inara Wali's footsteps grew lighter and her burdens began to lift, the ancient tree seemed to draw strength from her newfound resilience. Its gnarled bark softened, its branches reaching outward in a gesture of solidarity and support.

In that moment, amidst the quiet beauty of Malanga's sacred grove, Puttali Gachh stood as living evidence to the interconnectedness of all things. For as Inara Wali found solace and healing beneath its sheltering branches, so too did the tree itself find renewed purpose and vitality in her presence. And together, in harmony with the rhythms of the natural world, they whispered a silent prayer of gratitude to the universe for the gift of each new day.

6

Mahendra Park

In the heart of Malanga, nestled amidst the bustling town life, lay the tranquil sanctuary known as Mahendra Park, a homage to the revered King of Nepal. Enclosed by sturdy concrete walls, its modest entrance beckoned with a humble gate, inviting seekers of solace and community alike. Within its confines, a tapestry of purpose unfolded.

A stately hall stood, bearing witness to the deliberations of village panchayat members, their voices echoing with the weight of tradition and governance. Adjacent, a repository of knowledge resided, the library adorned with ancient scriptures and tales of yore, offering sanctuary to seekers of wisdom and imagination.

A haven for the elders awaited, a sanctuary where the retired denizens of society congregated, their leisurely pursuits imbued with the warmth of camaraderie and reminiscence. And beyond, a verdant expanse unfurled, a small field where the laughter of children danced in the golden glow of evening, their playful spirits weaving the very fabric of community beneath the watchful gaze of Mahendra Park.

In the heart of the park, where time sauntered and memories waltzed, a vivacious comportment of humanity unfolded each evening. Among the seasoned trees and the babbling breeze, the elderly graced the benches like custodians of a bygone era. With each dusk, they brought forth a treasure trove of narratives from the sanctum of their lives.

Some, with aching bones and weathered brows, lamented the relentless march of age, their voices carrying the weight of unspoken burdens. Others, with a twinkle in their eye, regaled listeners with tales of familial discord, a bystander to the intricacies of kinship. Amidst the laughter and occasional sighs, echoes of grandchildren's laughter danced like fireflies in the twilight.

Yet, amidst the mundane, there existed a cadre of daring souls, unabashed in their candour. They spoke of passions long past, of youthful dalliances and fervent desires that still pulsed within their aging hearts. Their words, though whispered, carried the spark of rebellion against time's relentless advance.

In the gathering dusk, some dared to flirt with the shadows, casting playful glances at passersby or bestowing mischievous compliments upon unsuspecting souls. In these fleeting moments, the park transformed into a theatre of secrets and desires, where age became but a fleeting whisper in the wind, and the heart remained ever youthful in its pursuit of connection and joy.

In the sun-dappled grip of the park, a mosaic of children, each woven from unique strands of life, gathered to play. Among them, a multiplicity of families unfolded, rich in diversity. Some children, adorned in the finery of privilege, frolicked with expensive sports gear, their laughter echoing through the air. Others, their attire threadbare, their steps tentative, observed from the sidelines, their longing palpable in the hushed whispers of their gaze.

Within the verdant canopy, where branches of trees reached out like welcoming arms, some found solace, swinging with carefree abandon. Meanwhile, delicate petals became tokens of joy, as children crafted moments of whimsy with nature's own treasures. Amid this kaleidoscope of play, a silent ache lingered—a yearning that transcended barriers of circumstance.

For those marginalized by fate's cruel hand—the impoverished, the differently abled, the ostracized—each moment was a demonstration to resilience in the face of exclusion. They served as silent spectators, their cheers a silent anthem of hope amidst the din of youthful exuberance. In their eyes, a silent plea echoed, longing to be woven into the fabric of belonging.

Yet, in life, helplessness knows no language, its shadows casting doubt upon the promise of tomorrow. For these children, there is no guiding light, no beacon of assurance to illuminate their path. Only the silent symphony of their collective longing, echoing through the corridors of time, pleading for a chance to dance amidst the sunlight of belonging.

As the Sun would go down, a bunch of grown up of boys and men from affluent families would visit the park and would tap the skint unfortunate girls to incite their humility. But the whole lot went un noticed. Those needy teenagers had barely any cloth on them. They could not afford or they did not know at all about all these. Some boys and men would offer them money or else while demanding for annoying favours. These all were a common and conventional repetitions because no one ever demurred them or the social formulas were not that prevalent. Inara Wali was one of such sufferers!

In the tranquillity of Mahendra Park, amidst the whispers of aging trees and the gentle hum of passing time, two figures stood out amongst the throngs of elderly visitors: Shri Ram Avatar Yadav and Shri Govind Paswan. Their journey together traced back to the hazy days of childhood, where they shared not just classrooms but the very essence of camaraderie. From the dusty corridors of their village school to the hallowed halls of higher education, their paths intertwined like vines, growing ever stronger with each passing year.

Marriage found them in the embrace of their familiar village, where their vows echoed against the backdrop of familiarity. As destiny would have it, they ventured into the noble profession of teaching, finding themselves side by side once more, this time shaping young minds in the corridors of the same school they once attended.

Shri Ram Avtar, with his mastery over the nuances of Secondary English, commanded respect and admiration from students and colleagues alike. Meanwhile, Shri Govind Paswan's teachings in the realm of Social Sciences painted vibrant tapestries of knowledge, enriching the minds of all who crossed his path.

Yet, beneath the facade of professionalism lay a bond forged in the fires of companionship. Theirs was a relationship painted in shades of love and brotherhood, woven with threads of togetherness that transcended the constraints of time.

But like any tale of kinship, theirs bore the scars of playful banter turned sour. Their jests, once shared in mirthful abandon, could sometimes ignite sparks of conflict, leading to heated exchanges and even physical altercations. In those moments, the air between them crackled with tension, their bond strained by the weight of misunderstanding.

Yet, like the ebb and flow of the tides, their discord was but a fleeting shadow in their friendship. For in the quiet moments of reflection, amidst the green expanse of Mahendra Park, reconciliation found its place. Like the first rays of dawn after a stormy night, they would come together once more, their laughter ringing through the air as if to proclaim that nothing could sever the ties that bound them.

In the heart of Mahendra Park, where the echoes of their laughter lingered long after they departed, the story of Shri Ram Avatar Yadav and Shri Govind Paswan remained a statement to the enduring power of friendship, where even the deepest rifts could be bridged by the simple grace of forgiveness.

In the heart of the park, where the sunlight danced through the leaves and painted the world with its golden hues, two souls of uncommon kindness dwelled. With keen eyes, they observed the young boys and girls who lingered at the sidelines, their longing gazes fixated on the joyous play of others. These children, bound by the chains of social detachment, seemed trapped in a realm of silent tales and unspoken despair.

Around twenty such souls graced the park with their presence, drawn by an unseen thread of hope. It was here that our compassionate duo, moved by empathy, decided to weave a new narrative. With hearts as generous as the dawn, they procured a football, a beacon of possibility amidst the shadows of despair. Gathering the children around them, they whispered promises of joy and invited them to partake in the game.

Oh, the ecstasy that lit up their faces! It was as if the weight of the world had been lifted, and in its place, pure elation blossomed. Yet, their benevolence knew no bounds. With each passing day, they nurtured the seeds of happiness, sowing fields of laughter and camaraderie. Contributions flowed like rivers of goodwill, enabling the purchase of more treasures: carrom boards, ludo sets, chess pieces—each a doorway to newfound delight.

Slowly but surely, the children shed their cloaks of invisibility, emerging from the shadows to embrace the light of possibility. No longer were they mere spectators, resigned to the sidelines of life. Instead, they became architects of their own joy, their laughter echoing like melodies through the park. Among them, one name shone like a beacon: Inara Wali, transformed by the kindness of two souls who dared to believe in the power of compassion.

In the gentle rhythm of rural life, a week unfolded its pages with a tranquil grace. Yet, amidst the muttering winds and rustling leaves, murmurs of dissent brewed in the heart of the village. There, beneath the sheltering boughs of ancient trees, a gathering of villagers convened to cast shadows upon the noble efforts of Shri Yadav and Paswan.

Their discontent found voice in complaints against the Village Panchayat Head, their accusations laden with veiled threats aimed at the very fabric of hope woven by the diligent teachers. Amidst the looming threat of dire consequences, whispered like ominous shadows in the ears of wary educators, the fragile dreams of children hung in the balance.

Faced with the daunting prospect of resistance at every turn, Yadav and Paswan, pillars of resilience, sought refuge in the sanctuary of ingenuity. They sought solace beneath the verdant canopy of Puttali Gachh, a haven untouched by the clamour of dissent.

Beneath the watchful gaze of ancient branches, a symbiotic dance unfolded each day. Children, their laughter a melodic symphony amidst the tranquil hum of grazing cattle, found respite and joy under the tutelage of Yadav and Paswan. Puttali Gachh, in its benevolence, bestowed its blessings upon the makeshift sanctuary, where hope flourished amidst adversity.

No longer mere figures of retirement, the teachers, rejuvenated by purpose, erected a humble abode beneath the protective embrace of Puttali Gachh. With the solemn nod of approval from the local guardians of order, their sanctuary became a beacon of resilience, weathering all seasons with steadfast resolve – be it the gentle caress of rain, the fierce embrace of hail, or the tumultuous fury of storm.

In the hushed confines of a humble classroom, where each stroke of chalk upon the blackboard articulated tales of diligence and dreams, a teacher meticulously etched out a lifeline of hope upon the canvas of time for a cadre of children. These young souls, beset by the harsh trials of scarcity – be it of resources, tender age, coin, or health – found themselves enveloped by an extraordinary backing of resilience and compassion.

Their educator, a custodian of both knowledge and empathy, recognized their invincible essence and sought to nurture it with a rare blend of altruism and opportunity. With a stroke of brilliance, a covenant was forged: for every hour spent poring over the pages of wisdom, an equal hour would be devoted to the sacred playground of childhood delight. Furthermore, the tools of enlightenment – books, notebooks, and stationery – would be bestowed upon them freely, erasing the barriers of economic constraint.

Word of this transformative decree spread like wildfire among the young scholars, who, in turn, imparted it to their guardians. And so, upon the dawn of the following morn, a procession of wary parents and guardians made pilgrimage to the hallowed abode of learning. Yet, within the creases of their furrowed brows and the scepticism lingering in their eyes, lay the remnants of countless shattered dreams and unfulfilled promises.

The task of persuasion lay heavy upon the shoulders of the educators, for they sought not merely to sway minds, but to rekindle the flickering flame of hope within hearts wearied by the unrelenting shadows of despair. Each syllable uttered was infused with the fervent belief that this initiative, however modest it may seem, heralded the dawn of a new era – a shelter where darkness found no refuge, and the promise of tomorrow beckoned with undiminished allure.

In the middle of the verdant cuddle of Puttali Gachh, joy danced upon its boughs as a thousand avian voices composed a symphony of celebration. Each leaf, a graceful dancer in the breeze, swayed in melodious rhythm, while the branches, like eager companions, reached out in exultation. Such a scene, a veritable benediction bestowed upon seekers of wisdom, custodians of knowledge, and architects of societal transformation.

In the nature beneath the sprawling branches of the Puttali Gachh, a sanctuary of learning blossomed under the dedicated efforts of Shri Ram Avatar and Shri Govind Paswan. Each dawn heralded a new harvest of achievements, as the children, inspired by their teachers' unwavering commitment, eagerly delved into the realms of knowledge.

In the face of countless obstacles, the inseparable pair tenaciously sought out fresh volumes and meticulously curated tailored lessons, deftly intertwining the rich fabric of scholarship with indispensable worldly knowledge and societal sagacity. What initially sparked as mere dalliance gracefully evolved into a meticulously structured pedagogical endeavour, with the al fresco classroom emerging as a luminous bastion of enlightenment for its ardent disciples.

Inara Wali and her companions, among the most receptive of scholars, absorbed the teachings with an unparalleled acumen, their minds akin to fertile soil eagerly imbibing the seeds of wisdom sown by their devoted mentors. Amidst the rigors of her daily life, Inara Wali encountered myriad challenges: cooking for her in-laws, fetching water for the family, tending to the grazing cattle, and preparing meals, all while navigating the obligatory social obligations of her community. Yet, despite these formidable obstacles, her unwavering commitment to learning shone through. Teachers, astounded by her academic prowess, leadership qualities, and profound thought processes, found in her a true intellectual luminary. Indeed, Inara Wali had constructed a towering edifice of thought-provoking inquiries, each knot in the fabric of her reformative questions a testament to her determined spirit. Recognizing her rapid academic growth, instructors bestowed upon her the utmost attention, nurturing her intellectual development with fervent dedication.

In the tranquil clinch of routine, a harmonious symphony echoed through the halls of the open-sky school. Here, amidst the boundless expanse of knowledge, both teachers and students found solace in their collective pursuit of enlightenment. The tale of their triumphs swiftly traversed the winds, igniting the village with whispers of their extraordinary journey.

Yet, amidst the jubilant echoes, a shadow lurked. The affluent denizens, ensconced in their privilege, viewed this blossoming bastion of education with disdain. To them, the prospect of an educated populace posed a threat to the status quo, disrupting the delicate balance of their domain. Who would tend to their fields, manage their households, or undertake the menial tasks they so abhorred? Simultaneously, a tremor of apprehension rippled through the hearts of the less fortunate. Would their children, once enlightened, face rejection from the very echelons they dared to aspire to? The prospect of unemployment loomed large, casting a pall over their aspirations.

In hushed tones, the affluent elite and their progeny conspired, weaving a drapery of dissent to sabotage the noble endeavour unfolding before them. In their clandestine machinations, a tale of opposition unfolded, threatening to cast a shadow over the hope that the open-sky school had become.

As the gentle light of dawn kissed the humble abode of learning, both teachers and students approached their sanctuary of knowledge, only to be greeted by a scene of disarray. Their once-sturdy hut stood dismantled, a testament to an act of unspeakable vandalism. Amidst the debris, a figure named Bhola Singh loomed, flanked by his cohorts brandishing menacing sticks. A child, swift and perceptive, darted away, a messenger of impending danger, racing to forewarn the educators of the imminent peril awaiting them.

Yet, in a twist of fate both tragic and courageous, the teachers, rather than evading the looming threat, strode boldly to confront it. A confrontation ensued, words clashing like swords in a battlefield of wills. With a flourish, Bhola Singh, his moustache bristling with defiance, cast a chilling gaze upon the educators, issuing a dire ultimatum. Two days, he declared, were all they had before consequences of unfathomable consequence would befall them, a warning etched with the weight of impending doom.

Despite repeated warnings, the teachers persisted in their usual routines, seemingly heedless of the looming threat. Bhola, a figure shrouded in infamy, cast a sinister shadow over the schoolyard. His methods were as crude as they were effective; he would intimidate students individually, employing his menacing cohorts to instil fear in the hearts of children. On numerous occasions, he would brazenly confront the teachers, resorting to physical aggression to assert his dominance. Yet, in the face of such adversity, the educators remained resolute and unwavering, their resolve unshaken by Bhola's nefarious actions. His misdeeds became the subject of gossip throughout the town, with many voices urging him to abandon his wicked ways. However, Bhola, consumed by his own hubris, revelled in his notoriety, proudly twirling his moustache as a symbol of his power. Such was the pervasive fear of Bhola that his mere presence instilled dread in all who crossed his path.

In the ethereal expanse of comprehension, students had begun to fathom the enigma: why does Bhola and his ilk harbour such fervent aggression towards the pursuit of education? Are they not endowed with the capacity to partake in erudition, to nurture minds refined enough to cultivate discerning opinions? Why must they be relegated solely to menial and ignoble tasks? What dictates their segregation, their exile from the bustling thoroughfares of societal centrality? No longer are they mere progeny or scholars; their cogitations have ascended to loftier realms, grappling with the weight of profound inquiries. For it is in the crucible of difficult questions that the crucible of progress is forged, be it at the individual, societal, or national echelon. Unified in purpose, they have metamorphosed into a cadre of reformists – stewards of change, luminaries ablaze with transformative ideas poised to imbue society afresh with notions of parity, equity, and boundless opportunity.

As the hands of time unfurled their ceaseless march, Bhola Singh's tyrannical shadow loomed larger with each passing day, casting a pall over the tranquil village of Inara Wali. Yet, amidst this sombre tableau, the stalwart resolve of the village teachers stood resolute, an unwavering beacon of hope amidst the encroaching darkness.

Undeterred by adversity, these unsung heroes continued their noble quest, imparting the invaluable gift of knowledge to eager young minds. Among them, Inara Wali emerged as a beacon of promise, her thirst for learning unquenchable. With each passing lesson, the mysteries of English and Nepalese language unveiled themselves before her, like blossoming petals in the dawn's embrace.

Guided by the sage wisdom of her mentors, Inara Wali ventured beyond the confines of mere academia, delving into the rich tapestry of literary treasures they shared. Through the pages of reformative literature, she found not only solace but enlightenment, her once fledgling intellect now soaring to new heights with each turn of the page. As the tendrils of knowledge intertwined with her being, a metamorphosis ensued, transmuting the very essence of her being. No longer confined by the limitations of her situation, Inara Wali's demeanour exuded an aura of cultivated refinement. Her attire, once humble, now bespoke a sophistication befitting a true scholar, while her eloquence and penmanship rivalled that of the most erudite minds.

Inara Wali, once a mere inhabitant of a remote village, now stood as a testament to the transformative power of education, her journey a testament to the spirited disposition of the human soul.

In the hallowed halls of Puttali Gacch, where the whispers of wisdom mingled with the echoes of hardship, there unfolded a saga of relentless cruelty orchestrated by the enigmatic Bhola Singh. Within this ancient institution, teachers stood as pillars of resilience, their endurance etched in the very fabric of their being, while learners navigated the web of knowledge, their aspirations intertwined with the drapery of fate.

Amidst this tableau of scholarly pursuits and human intricacies, Puttali Gacch emerged as a silent observer, bearing witness to the receding tide and flow of existence. With a keen eye that surpassed the comprehension of mere mortals, it beheld the intricate dance of destiny, mapping the trajectory of knowledge, efforts, and destinies alike.

In the sacred sanctum of learning, where each step reverberated with the weight of centuries past, Puttali

Gacch stood as a sentry of enlightenment, a silent scout amidst the tempest of life's trials and triumphs.

7
Affluent's Opposition Unfolds

In the nature beneath the sprawling branches of the Puttali Gachh, a sanctuary of learning blossomed under the dedicated efforts of Shri Ram Avatar and Shri Govind Paswan. Each dawn heralded a new harvest of achievements, as the children, inspired by their teachers' unwavering commitment, eagerly delved into the realms of knowledge.

In the face of countless obstacles, the inseparable pair tenaciously sought out fresh volumes and meticulously curated tailored lessons, deftly intertwining the rich fabric of scholarship with indispensable worldly knowledge and societal sagacity. What initially sparked as mere dalliance gracefully evolved into a meticulously structured pedagogical endeavour, with the al fresco classroom emerging as a luminous bastion of enlightenment for its ardent disciples.

Inara Wali and her companions, among the most receptive of scholars, absorbed the teachings with an unparalleled acumen, their minds akin to fertile soil eagerly imbibing the seeds of wisdom sown by their devoted mentors. Amidst the rigors of her daily life, Inara Wali encountered myriad challenges: cooking for her in-laws, fetching water for the family, tending to the grazing cattle, and preparing meals, all while navigating the obligatory social obligations of her community. Yet, despite these formidable obstacles, her unwavering commitment to learning shone through. Teachers, astounded by her academic prowess, leadership qualities, and profound thought processes, found in her a true intellectual luminary. Indeed, Inara Wali had constructed a towering edifice of thought-provoking inquiries, each knot in the fabric of her reformative questions a testament to her determined spirit. Recognizing her rapid academic growth, instructors bestowed upon her the utmost attention, nurturing her intellectual development with fervent dedication.

In the tranquil clinch of routine, a harmonious symphony echoed through the halls of the open-sky school. Here, amidst the boundless expanse of knowledge, both teachers and students found solace in their collective pursuit of enlightenment. The tale of their triumphs swiftly traversed the winds, igniting the village with whispers of their extraordinary journey.

Yet, amidst the jubilant echoes, a shadow lurked. The affluent denizens, ensconced in their privilege, viewed this blossoming bastion of education with disdain. To them, the prospect of an educated populace posed a threat to the status quo, disrupting the delicate balance of their domain. Who would tend to their fields, manage their households, or undertake the menial tasks they so abhorred?

Simultaneously, a tremor of apprehension rippled through the hearts of the less fortunate. Would their children, once enlightened, face rejection from the very echelons they dared to aspire to? The prospect of unemployment loomed large, casting a pall over their aspirations.

In hushed tones, the affluent elite and their progeny conspired, weaving a drapery of dissent to sabotage the noble endeavour unfolding before them. In their clandestine machinations, a tale of opposition unfolded, threatening to cast a shadow over the hope that the open-sky school had become.

As the gentle light of dawn kissed the humble abode of learning, both teachers and students approached their sanctuary of knowledge, only to be greeted by a scene of disarray. Their once-sturdy hut stood dismantled, a testament to an act of unspeakable vandalism. Amidst the debris, a figure named Bhola Singh loomed, flanked by his cohorts brandishing menacing sticks. A child, swift and perceptive, darted away, a messenger of impending danger, racing to forewarn the educators of the imminent peril awaiting them.

Yet, in a twist of fate both tragic and courageous, the teachers, rather than evading the looming threat, strode boldly to confront it. A confrontation ensued, words clashing like swords in a battlefield of wills. With a flourish, Bhola Singh, his moustache bristling with defiance, cast a chilling gaze upon the educators, issuing a dire ultimatum. Two days, he declared, were all they had before consequences of unfathomable consequence would befall them, a warning etched with the weight of impending doom.

Despite repeated warnings, the teachers persisted in their usual routines, seemingly heedless of the looming threat. Bhola, a figure shrouded in infamy, cast a sinister shadow over the schoolyard. His methods were as crude as they were effective; he would intimidate students individually, employing his menacing cohorts to instil fear in the hearts of children. On numerous occasions, he would brazenly confront the teachers, resorting to physical aggression to assert his dominance. Yet, in the face of such adversity, the educators remained resolute and unwavering, their resolve unshaken by Bhola's nefarious actions. His misdeeds became the subject of gossip throughout the town, with many voices urging him to abandon his wicked ways. However, Bhola, consumed by his own hubris, revelled in his notoriety, proudly twirling his moustache as a symbol of his power. Such was the pervasive fear of Bhola that his mere presence instilled dread in all who crossed his path.

In the ethereal expanse of comprehension, students had begun to fathom the enigma: why does Bhola and his ilk harbour such fervent aggression towards the pursuit of education? Are they not endowed with the capacity to partake in erudition, to nurture minds refined enough to cultivate discerning opinions? Why must they be relegated solely to menial and ignoble tasks? What dictates their segregation, their exile from the bustling thoroughfares of societal centrality?

No longer are they mere progeny or scholars; their cogitations have ascended to loftier realms, grappling with the weight of profound inquiries. For it is in the crucible of difficult questions that the crucible of progress is forged, be it at the individual, societal, or national echelon. Unified in purpose, they have metamorphosed into a cadre of reformists – stewards of change, luminaries ablaze with transformative ideas poised to imbue society afresh with notions of parity, equity, and boundless opportunity.

As the hands of time unfurled their ceaseless march, Bhola Singh's tyrannical shadow loomed larger with each passing day, casting a pall over the tranquil village of Inara Wali. Yet, amidst this sombre tableau, the stalwart resolve of the village teachers stood resolute, an unwavering beacon of hope amidst the encroaching darkness.

Undeterred by adversity, these unsung heroes continued their noble quest, imparting the invaluable gift of knowledge to eager young minds. Among them, Inara Wali emerged as a beacon of promise, her thirst for learning unquenchable. With each passing lesson, the mysteries of English and Nepalese language unveiled themselves before her, like blossoming petals in the dawn's embrace.

Guided by the sage wisdom of her mentors, Inara Wali ventured beyond the confines of mere academia, delving into the rich tapestry of literary treasures they shared. Through the pages of reformative literature, she found not only solace but enlightenment, her once fledgling intellect now soaring to new heights with each turn of the page. As the tendrils of knowledge intertwined with her being, a metamorphosis ensued, transmuting the very essence of her being. No longer confined by the limitations of her station, Inara Wali's demeanour exuded an aura of cultivated refinement. Her attire, once humble, now bespoke a sophistication befitting a true scholar, while her eloquence and penmanship rivalled that of the most erudite minds.

Inara Wali, once a mere inhabitant of a remote village, now stood as a testament to the transformative power of education, her journey a testament to the spirited disposition of the human soul.

In the hallowed halls of Puttali Gacch, where the whispers of wisdom mingled with the echoes of hardship, there unfolded a saga of relentless cruelty orchestrated by the enigmatic Bhola Singh. Within this ancient institution, teachers stood as pillars of resilience, their endurance etched in the very fabric of their being, while learners navigated the web of knowledge, their aspirations intertwined with the drapery of fate.

Amidst this tableau of scholarly pursuits and human intricacies, Puttali Gacch emerged as a silent observer, bearing witness to the receding tide and flow of existence. With a keen eye that surpassed the comprehension of mere mortals, it beheld the intricate dance of destiny, mapping the trajectory of knowledge, efforts, and destinies alike.

In the sacred sanctum of learning, where each step reverberated with the weight of centuries past, Puttali Gacch stood as a sentry of enlightenment, a silent scout amidst the tempest of life's trials and triumphs.

8

Rise of Inara Wali

In the ethereal arras of Shri Ram Avatar and Shri Govind Paswan's world, there existed a gem of unparalleled brilliance: Inara Wali. Her talents, scrutinized by the discerning gaze of these esteemed figures, yearned for recognition beyond their approval. At the age of twenty-four, she exuded a captivating allure. Her eyes, a mesmerizing flare, beckoned admirers, while her partly curly locks framed a countenance of enchanting beauty. Tall and slender, she moved with the grace of a swan, her every step imbued with celestial elegance. A perpetual smile graced her lips, accentuating the delicate curve of her thin mouth. Embracing a newfound sense of agency, she tended to her appearance with care, her in-laws mirroring her transformation with offerings of fine garments and the gift of autonomy. In this tableau of evolving grace, Inara Wali emerged as a radiant embodiment of feminine splendour, awaiting her moment to shine in the spotlight of acclaim.

In the realm of her daily existence, amidst the humble chores of cooking, fetching water, and tending to the grazing cattle, she wove a of grace and dignity. Each task, however modest, was imbued with a sense of purpose and belonging, as she embraced them with unwavering pride. To her, they were not mere trifles, but threads in the fabric of her life, each stitch sewn with reverence and ownership.

Yet, amidst the backdrop of her daily toils, there existed a magnetism that drew the gaze of young boys, regardless of their situation in life. Whether affluent or of humbler means, she held sway over their hearts, a vision of femininity and allure that transcended social boundaries.

Despite the weight of her widowhood, she bore her burden with an unyielding spirit, never allowing herself to forget the reality of her circumstances. Her mind, enriched by the gift of education, soared beyond the confines of her daily routine, her thoughts traversing vast horizons of knowledge and insight. She remained steadfast in her pursuit of enlightenment, her thirst for wisdom unquenchable as she turned the pages of countless volumes, each word a tribute to her unconquerable spirit and unwavering fortitude.

In the annals of Nepalese society, "The Rising Nepal" – an English daily -stood as a sign of enlightenment, its pages whispering truths to the ears of the privileged few. Revered for its unyielding commitment to amplifying the voices of the people, it served as a conduit between the populace and the monarchy of yore. Within its editorial sanctum, profound discussions on the bedrock issues of society unfurled wisdom, each word a brushstroke crafting a lesson for the ages.

Amidst this intellectual oasis, Inara Wali found solace and inspiration. Gifted with the sustenance of knowledge by the benevolence of Shri Ram Avatar, she delved into the depths of "The Rising Nepal" with fervour, absorbing its every word as though each syllable were a drop of nectar for her burgeoning intellect. Regularly, she convened with her mentors and fellow seekers of truth in the hallowed halls of the open sky school, engaging in spirited debates fuelled by the insights gleaned from the newspaper's pages.

With each passing day, Inara Wali's mind unfurled like a lotus in bloom, its petals reaching towards the sun of enlightenment. Through the discourse fostered by "The Rising Nepal," she honed her voice, readying herself to join the symphony of intellects shaping the destiny of a nation.

Amidst the gentle rustle of Kathmandu's ancient streets, a whispered promise fluttered through the pages of a newspaper: "Social Opportunity for all." Inara Wali, her spirit alight with the tantalizing prospect, felt a fervent desire kindle within her. Yet, the dream seemed as distant as the mountain peaks that cradled her homeland of Malanga.

In the hushed corners of determination, her teachers became the silent architects of her ambition, their unwavering support a beacon amidst the shadows of doubt. Yet, the path ahead seemed shrouded in impossibility, a labyrinth of obstacles veiling the possibility of her ascent.

Summoning courage like a monarch rallying her court, the teachers beseeched the aid of Inara Wali's in-laws, seeking passage through the fortress of financial constraints. But alas, the coffers lay barren, save for a flicker of hope that danced upon the lips of her father-in-law, who, though lacking in wealth, offered a pact: if she were to journey forth, her mother-in-law must be her steadfast companion. With resources as scarce as whispers in the wind, the teachers, too, felt the weight of their limitations. Yet, in the crucible of dedication, a sacrifice was made as one teacher pledged his treasured ring to the cause, a symbol of commitment forged in the fires of determination.

And so, with dreams packed neatly alongside necessities, they embarked upon a pilgrimage of perseverance, their journey a corroboration to the invincible spirit that knows no bounds. From the dust-laden streets of Malanga to the bustling thoroughfares of Kathmandu, their passage was a resilience and fortitude.

Crossing borders both literal and figurative, they traversed valleys and plains, guided by the flickering flame of aspiration that illuminated their path. And as night descended like a velvet curtain upon their weary frames, they found solace in the embrace of a Dharamsala, the chill of winter's breath tempered by the warmth of camaraderie.

Yet, as slumber claimed their weary bodies, the teachers lingered in the realm of wakefulness, their minds awash with apprehension. For Inara Wali was not merely a participant in this grand symphony of opportunity; she was the embodiment of their hopes, their efforts, their sacrifices—a fragile vessel entrusted with the weight of their dreams. And in the quiet hours of introspection, they grappled with the spectre of inadequacy, haunted by the fear of failure and the sting of potential defeat.

But beneath the robe of uncertainty, a flame flickered—a flame fuelled not by the brilliance of intellect or the weight of experience, but by the purity of intention and the resilience of the human spirit. And as dawn's first light pierced the veil of night, illuminating the horizon with the promise of a new day, they rose to meet the challenges that awaited, their hearts buoyed by the unwavering belief that within the heart of every obstacle lies the seed of opportunity, waiting to bloom.

As the clock struck 11 AM, they graced the venue with their presence, each figure adorned in the elegance of formal attire. Among them, Inara Wali stood out, draped in a resplendent blue sari, adorned with intricate silver embroidery—a garment once cherished by the wife of Shri Ram Avatar. Shri Govind Paswan, in his own right, brought forth the radiance of his wife's jewellery, a tribute to her grace and beauty. With meticulous care, his mother-in-law adorned herself with makeup, enhancing her already captivating features.

With an air of reality, she entered the hall, each step a substantiation to her poise, her exotic smile illuminating the room as she gracefully turned her long neck. All eyes in the hall turned to behold her, captivated by her presence. With humility and grace, she extended her greetings to all, her hands folded in reverence, before settling into the seat designated for her in the first row, second chair, as meticulously arranged by the organizers.

As the event commenced, teachers and the esteemed mother-in-law occupied the audience gallery, their presence lending an aura of wisdom and admiration to the gathering.

In the grand theatre of anticipation, amidst a sea of eager faces, the anchor gracefully ushered in a moment of profound significance. With a voice that resonated with authority, her words echoed with unwavering certainty as she beckoned forth the esteemed judges, the spirited participants, and the cherished audience. Yet, it was a transformative crescendo that ensued when her tone, once gentle, now swelled with fervour and resolve, as she heralded the next speaker. "Now, may I humbly request the presence of Ms. Sujata from Malanga to grace us with her words," she proclaimed. And then, with a flourish of admiration, she revealed a truth that stirred the collective soul: "Ladies and gentlemen, prepare to be uplifted, for this remarkable soul, Sujata, shines bright in our midst despite the absence of formal education—no schooling, no college. Yet, she stands here, an authentication to the steadfast essence that dwells within. Ladies and gentlemen, I present to you, Sujata...!"

And Sujata Speaks....!

Ladies and gentlemen,

Imagine a garden where seeds are scattered haphazardly, where some fall on fertile soil while others land on rocky ground or among thorns. In this garden, the seeds represent the potential within each of us, while the varying conditions symbolize the circumstances into which we are born. Some seeds may sprout and flourish, blessed by favourable conditions and nurturing care. Others may struggle to survive, weighed down by the challenges they face.

I stand before you today as a seed that fell on rocky ground, deprived of the nutrients and support needed to thrive. My journey has been one of adversity and hardship, marked by poverty, discrimination, and lack of formal education. But like the resilient seedling that pushes through the cracks in the rock, I refused to let my circumstances define me. I refused to accept that my fate was sealed by the conditions into which I was born.

In the parable of the garden, we see a reflection of our society—a society where social opportunity is not distributed equally, where some are blessed with privilege while others are left to fend for themselves. But just as a gardener tends to his garden, nurturing each seed regardless of where it falls, so too must we tend to the social fabric of our society, ensuring that every individual has the opportunity to thrive.

At its core, the philosophy of social opportunity for all is rooted in the belief that every person has inherent worth and potential, regardless of their background or circumstances. It is a recognition that talent and ability are not confined to the privileged few, but are found in every corner of society, waiting to be discovered and cultivated. But achieving social opportunity for all requires more than just good intentions; it requires action. It requires us to break down the barriers that stand in the way of progress, whether they be economic, social, or institutional. It requires us to invest in education, healthcare, and social services, providing the support and resources needed for every individual to reach their full potential.

Moreover, it requires a shift in mindset—a recognition that true progress is not measured solely by material wealth or status, but by the well-being and empowerment of every member of society. It requires us to embrace the principles of inclusivity, empathy, and solidarity, recognizing that we are all interconnected and that the success of one is bound up with the success of all. As a society, we cannot afford to leave anyone behind. We cannot ignore the voices of the marginalized and disenfranchised. We must strive for a future where social opportunity is not a luxury afforded to a privileged few, but a fundamental right guaranteed to all.

So let us come together, not as strangers divided by our differences, but as fellow human beings united in our pursuit of a better tomorrow. Let us build a world where social opportunity is not just a lofty ideal, but a lived reality for every individual, regardless of their past or present circumstances.

In closing, let us not be content to live in a society where social opportunity is a privilege reserved for the few. Let us strive instead for a world where every individual, regardless of their background or circumstances, has the chance to flourish and thrive. Let us tend to the garden of society with care and compassion, ensuring that no seed is left to wither and die, but that all may blossom into the fullness of their potential.

Thank you.

Amidst a crescendo of applause, the grand hall enveloped in its embrace every soul present—judges, participants, dignitaries, and enraptured audiences alike—all remained standing in reverent admiration until she gracefully returned to her designated place. With a serene exhale, she savoured a sip of water, her eyes alight with gratitude as she exchanged warm smiles with the mentors and her cherished mother-in-law.

Her eloquent speech, a masterpiece of sincerity and conviction, resonated far and wide as it danced through the airwaves, carried by the waves of radio transmission. With the dawn of the following morning, the printed pages of newspapers blossomed with extracts of her impassioned discourse, adorned with her likeness captured in a moment of triumph. Each word of her speech, delicate yet fortified with unwavering resolve, echoed the depths of her convictions, stirring hearts and minds alike.

Inara Wali's ascent, a testament to resilience and determination, unfurled before the eyes of the world—a narrative woven intricately, whether through the tapestry of rags to riches or the enduring yields of the nurturing guidance bestowed upon her by her revered teachers.

9

Towns' Talk – Hope Awakens

In the quaint confines of the town, a whisper took flight, born of the tongue of Bhola Singh, a harbinger of tales both beguiling and bitter. With the skill of a weaver, he spun a narrative that cast shadows upon the honour of Inara Wali, painting her flight from the midst as a clandestine affair, orchestrated by none other than her own revered mentors. Ignorance, that eternal shroud, cloaked the minds of those who lent their ears to Bhola's lamentations, shielding them from the rays of truth that illuminated Inara Wali's path to fame. For these souls knew not the symphony of the radio waves, nor did they tread the paths of enlightenment offered by the printed word.

In their ignorance, they became the unwitting pawns in a dark game, marshalled by Bhola and his ilk to sow seeds of discord and disdain. The sanctity of those venerable teachers' abodes was violated by the storm of indignation that swept through the streets, fuelled by the flames of hearsay and the tempest of unchecked emotions. A gathering, not of unity but of malevolence, congregated with sinister intent, their hearts set upon a course of violence against those who had nurtured the mind and soul of Inara Wali.

Such was the power of rumour, that it sculpted reality in its own twisted image, casting innocence as guilt and virtue as vice. And thus, amidst the tumult of tongues and the clamour of discontent, Bhola Singh and his cabal etched their mark upon the annals of the town's history, their names whispered with equal parts fear and fervour, as the talk of the town reached a crescendo of chaos and calamity.

In the heart of Malanga, where the winds carried whispers of tradition and the sun casted its golden glow upon fields of wheat, there returned a figure of noble stature. Mahesh, freshly adorned with the laurels of a master's degree in Political Science, graced the town with his presence once more. With a complexion kissed by the sun's embrace, he stood tall and sturdy, his frame sculpted like that of an athlete. Yet, it was his azure gaze that captivated all who dared meet his eyes, imbued with the wisdom of ages and the fervour of a scholar.

As the brother of Mukhiya Jee's second wife, Mahesh found solace in the familial hug upon his return, tethering himself to the familiar clinch of home. Raised amidst the very fabric of Malanga's, he bore witness to its intricacies, the ebb and flow of its people, their customs, and their social ethos. From his earliest days, Mahesh espoused the creed of liberalism, a flare of dissent against the injustices that plagued the underprivileged.

His voice, a clarion call for social justice, resounded through the cobblestone streets, challenging norms and stirring the conscience of those who would heed. Such convictions, however noble, oftentimes brought tumult to the doorstep of Mukhiya Jee, a burden not lightly borne. Thus, it was decided that Mahesh should seek enlightenment afar, sent to distant lands to cultivate his intellect, to shield both himself and the esteemed Mukhiya Jee from further strife.

Yet, like the river that knows no bounds, Mahesh's return heralded a new chapter in the annals of Malanga. His education, a vessel brimming with knowledge, now anchored him to the soil he called home. Un - swayed by the allure of fleeting romances or the siren song of worldly pleasures, Mahesh devoted himself wholly to pursuits of the mind. In his study, he found sanctuary, labouring tirelessly to transmute his ideals into tangible deeds, to sculpt a world more just and equitable with each turn of the page.

Thus, in the heart of Malanga, amidst the whispers of tradition and the rustle of the wheat fields, stood Mahesh - a scholar, a champion of the marginalized, and a harbinger of change.

In Mahendar Park, whispers carried tales swiftly, weaving a tale of secrets and schemes. Amongst these murmurs, Mahesh stumbled upon the clandestine plans of Bhola Singh and his cohorts. With a heart laden with concern, Mahesh endeavoured to steer them from their course, offering counsel born from a wellspring of goodwill. Yet, his efforts were met with stern rebuke, as Bhola Singh's faction, veiled in a cloak of defiance, dismissed his entreaties, warning him to tread cautiously and abstain from entangling himself in their affairs.

Perplexed and disheartened, Mahesh found himself at a crossroads, grappling with the weight of his conscience and the urgency of the situation. Seeking solace and guidance, he turned to the venerable Mukhiya Jee, a sign of wisdom in the community. With bated breath, Mahesh laid bare the unfolding narrative, awaiting the sage counsel of the village elder.

In a silence that stretched across the expanse of an hour, Mukhiya Jee, with furrowed brow and measured contemplation, absorbed the gravity of the revelation. Words hung in the air, heavy with implication, yet Mukhiya Jee remained reticent, offering neither affirmation nor dissent.

As the sun dipped below the horizon, casting long shadows across the village square, Mukhiya Jee's decree resonated through the tranquil evening air. A summon to Mahendar Park echoed forth, calling upon the villagers to convene for a panchayat meeting of profound significance. With a sense of purpose and anticipation, the denizens gathered at Mahendar park, their hearts stirred by the promise of resolution and the dawning of a new chapter in their collective tale.

As the first rays of dawn gently caressed the sleepy town, a subtle anticipation stirred in the air, whispered by the rhythmic beats of four drummers dispatched to herald an imminent event. With the sun's ascent, the slumbering town awoke, not merely in body but in spirit and wisdom, drawn to the magnetic pull of an undisclosed gathering.

Overnight, the landscape transformed, bustling with eager souls converging upon the heart of Mahendar Park, their curiosity piqued by the sudden emergence of loudspeakers, harbingers of an enigmatic assembly. Yet, amidst the clamour and conjecture, a hush fell like a sacred veil as Mukhiya Jee, a figure of authority and reverence, took his place before the expectant multitude.

With a voice that resonated with command, Mukhiya Jee broke the silence, extending his apologies for the abrupt summons, acknowledging the lack of prior disclosure. In his address, he unveiled a tale of triumph, weaving a narrative of courage and perseverance embodied by one of their own: Inara Wali, a widow whose journey from obscurity to acclaim illuminated the path of hope.

Inara Wali's ascent, nurtured under the tutelage of Shri Ram Avatar and Shri Govind Paswan, bore testament to the transformative power of education. Escorted by her devoted mother-in-law and revered mentors, she ventured to Kathmandu, where her indomitable spirit captured the pinnacle of success, securing the coveted first position in a prestigious seminar.

Mukhiya Jee's words painted a portrait of admiration for Inara Wali, extolling her diligence and resilience amid adversity. The echo of her triumph reverberated beyond the confines of Mahendar Park, gracing the pages of newspapers adorned with her radiant visage.

In the wake of her achievement, the Panchayat, moved by a sense of communal pride, resolved to honour not only Inara Wali but also her benevolent teachers, whose unwavering support paved the path to glory. In a gesture of gratitude, the Panchayat pledged to shoulder their financial burdens, ensuring their sacrifices did not go unnoticed or unreciprocated.

As the sun cast its benevolent gaze upon the gathered throng, Mukhiya Jee concluded with an invitation, a beacon of unity and celebration. Tomorrow, beneath the verdant shade of Puttali Gachh, at the appointed hour of 3:00 PM, the community would unite in a symphony of welcome, extending their collective admiration to Inara Wali and her revered mentors, a testament to the enduring spirit of resilience and solidarity that bound them together.

In the quaint corners of the town, undertones swayed upon the breeze, carrying tales of Inara Wali and her sage mentors, stirring the hearts of all who heard. Anger, like a tempest, brewed among the people, directed at Bhola Singh and his comrades, their actions laid bare for all to see. The narrative, once hidden in shadows, now basked in the limelight, becoming the pulse of every conversation, the marrow of every gathering.

Men, amidst the verdant fields, found solace in shared murmurs, while women, in their daily toils, wove the fabric of their discourse with threads of curiosity and concern. Through each exchange, a concerto of emotions swirled, painting the town in hues of anticipation and longing.

Yet, amidst the hubbub, there arose ideal of faith, a lifeline for those who had yearned for a glimmer of possibility. Their dreams, nurtured in the soil of patience, now blossomed into reality. Like seeds carried on the wind, the message traversed far and wide, igniting flames of optimism in even the most distant hearts.

In the hushed corridors of societal hierarchy, her triumph cast shadows of discomfort upon more than just the Bhola Singh faction. Among the ranks of the affluent, her ascent was not hailed with jubilation, but rather met with whispered murmurs of dissent. To them, her success was not merely an individual accolade; it was a brazen affront, a challenge issued by a woman of humble origins to the entrenched privileges of their pedigrees. In the quiet recesses of their opulent estates, they harboured a steadfast allegiance to the antiquated norms of social stratification, recoiling at any notion of equitable opportunity that dared to disturb the delicate equilibrium of their status quo.

In the midst of this silent dissent, Mukhiya Jee loomed as a formidable bastion of tradition, a towering figure whose wealth and influence brooked no challenge within the village. And so, despite their disquietude, they chose the path of passive acquiescence, preserving the veneer of harmony while beneath it simmered the simmering cauldron of ideological conflict, a battle that had raged through the annals of time.

Amidst the clash of opposing ideologies, a profound truth emerged: these entrenched beliefs, knitted into the very frame of society, had long been the shackles that bound millions to live bereft of basic necessities – education, healthcare, sustenance, and dignity. Generations had languished in the grip of deprivation, their aspirations stifled by the unyielding grip of tradition.

For those who dared to dream of a different tomorrow, her triumph marked the dawn of a new era, a glimmer of hope amidst the darkness of oppression. But for those entrenched in their dogmas, it spelled naught but conspiracy – a threat to the foundations upon which their privilege was built. Thus, amidst the cacophony of conflicting ideals, a silent struggle unfolded, echoing the eternal tug-of-war between progress and tradition.

At precisely 3:00 PM the following day, as arranged, Mukhiya Jee orchestrated a grand celebration. The air was alive with the vibrant sounds of dhol and shehnai, while garlands of roses, jasmine, and marigolds added splashes of colour to the scene. All the town's dignitaries were in attendance, and a notable presence from the local police lent an air of formality to the occasion.

The gathering was a diverse area of the community: ladies, gentlemen, and children from less affluent backgrounds stood together, slightly apart from the affluent attendees. The turnout among the affluent was sparse, yet those who did come were spirited, well-educated, and from respectable families.

Inara Wali, along with her mother-in-law and the teachers, initially felt a pang of apprehension at the sight of the large crowd. They hesitated at the periphery, unsure of the crowd's intentions. Sensing their hesitation, several men and women crossed over to reassure them, explaining that the assembly was there to honour and welcome them. With their fears allayed, Inara Wali and her companions stepped forward, met by a reception of pomp and ceremony. Mukhiya Jee and the dignitaries greeted them with kind and gracious words, making them feel truly cherished. The atmosphere brimmed with unrestrained joy, leaving no doubt of the community's heartfelt welcome.

10

Open Sky School Success

Time flowed on, and the fervour and whispers surrounding her triumph gradually faded into the background. Life returned to its routine cadence. The school for the downtrodden, still under the aegis of Puttali Gacch, continued to operate, welcoming students from various backgrounds. The teachers, now seasoned by their achievements, remained humble, earning the deep respect of the community. Yet, Bhola Singh persisted in his disruptive ways. He relentlessly menaced both students and teachers, concocting schemes to hinder the students' journey to the school and creating obstacles for the teachers in their noble mission.

Inspired by the triumphant narrative of Inara Wali, a group of affluent families approached the dedicated teachers of the school with an enticing proposition. They suggested that the teachers cease their current endeavours and instead educate their children. To sweeten the deal, they offered a superior venue, complete with state-of-the-art infrastructure, and promised generous salaries.

However, the teachers, unwavering in their commitment to equality, proposed a counteroffer. They would accept the new arrangement on the condition that children from lower castes were also permitted to join the prestigious venue. This condition incensed the affluent families, who stormed away, threatening the teachers in their frustration.

In retaliation, the affluent families chose to punish the teachers through social ostracism. Invitations to social events such as weddings and prayer meetings ceased, and the teachers and their families were treated as social outcasts, much like the marginalized communities they sought to support. The teachers, with keen understanding, perceived the silent punishment, as did their families, who displayed remarkable solidarity and resilience.

Despite the social neglect and the personal pain that accompanied it, the teachers and their families stood firm in their principles and virtues. Their courage and steadfastness in the face of adversity were a testament to their character. In them, one could see the embodiment of divine virtue, as if they were sent by a higher power to champion the cause of justice and equality.

Many Panchayat Heads from nearby villages approached Mukhiya Jee with a heartfelt request: to allow students from their villages to join the thriving educational gatherings. Mukhiya Jee, ever compassionate, urged the teachers to welcome these eager children. Consequently, the number of students gathering beneath the majestic Puttali Gacch steadily grew, transforming the scene into a vibrant assembly of youthful energy and scholarly pursuit under the open sky. For three hours each day, except on Saturdays (Saturday being a weekly holiday in Nepal), the children engaged in a joyful routine. They played freely, danced with abandon, sang to their hearts' content, and immersed themselves in the lessons meticulously designed by their dedicated teachers. The lively interaction between students and teachers painted a picture of a flourishing educational community.

However, as the numbers swelled, the challenge of managing the expenses for such a large group became increasingly daunting. The teachers faced numerous difficulties: the need for additional manpower, essential amenities such as books, notebooks, pencils, pens, drawing tools, a blackboard, a duster, and chalk. Moreover, classrooms were essential to shield the children from the capricious weather. Many students arrived hungry, and there was not enough food to share, adding to the distress.

These burdens weighed heavily on the teachers, prompting them to approach Mukhiya Jee and share the struggles they faced in providing education to this ever-growing number of students. Mukhiya Jee had not foreseen the extent of these challenges when he had graciously allowed students from other villages, fulfilling the requests of his fellow Mukhiyas.

Seeking contributions from the other villages was a possible solution, yet it conflicted with Mukhiya Jee's sense of pride. He stood at a crossroads, needing to find a way to sustain this noble educational endeavour without compromising his principles or the welfare of the children and their devoted teachers.

Mukhiya Jee, initially resolved to support the open sky school through his own means, soon realized the wisdom in involving the village's affluent residents. He understood that their recognition and partnership would be crucial for the venture's success. To this end, he called for a gathering of all the affluent villagers in the hall of Mahendar Park. Among the invitees were also the teachers, Mahesh and Inara Wali.

In preparation, Mukhiya Jee had instructed the teachers to ensure that Inara Wali would explain the school's importance and needs to the village dignitaries, seeking their support. The following afternoon, the hall of Mahendar Park filled with the invited guests. Inara Wali, dressed in her best available sari, chose a seat in a rear corner of the hall, aware that the affluent guests might not appreciate her sitting among them. Her sari and blouse, less impressive than those she wore at the seminar, did not draw attention. She sat barefoot, modestly covering her mouth and face, feeling a mix of nervousness, fear, and contemplation about the outcome of this gathering.

As everyone settled, Mukhiya Jee opened with a brief speech. Shri Ram Avatar then took the floor, informing the audience about the school's progress and its significant impact. He concluded by inviting Inara Wali to appeal to the community for their charitable support to sustain the educational initiative. Inara Wali rose, and with a heart full of determination, began her address to the assembled dignitaries.

Honourable Members of the Village Panchayat, Esteemed Elders, and Respected Guests, Today, I stand before you with a heart full of hope and a story of remarkable success that has blossomed under the humble branches of the Puttalli Gacch. Our open sky school, despite its modest beginnings, has become a beacon of learning and a symbol of what can be achieved with determination and community spirit.

In a world where the lack of infrastructure often impedes progress, our school stands as a testament to the power of passion and perseverance. We have no formal classrooms, no sophisticated teaching amenities, and a limited number of dedicated teachers. Yet, against all odds, our school is thriving. Students from neighbouring villages are joining in numbers that exceed our expectations, eager to learn and grow in an environment that, while lacking in physical resources, is rich in enthusiasm and commitment.

This success, however, brings with it new challenges. The influx of students highlights the urgent need for better resources—adequate shelter from the elements, proper teaching materials, and more educators to nurture these bright young minds. It is here that we humbly seek your support. Your charitable contributions can make an immense difference. By investing in this initiative, you will not only be providing immediate aid but also planting the seeds for a brighter future. Education is the cornerstone of progress, and by uplifting the downtrodden, you are creating a foundation for sustained community growth and prosperity.

Imagine a future where every child in our village, regardless of their background, has the opportunity to learn, to dream, and to achieve. Education empowers individuals with the knowledge and skills they need to improve their lives and contribute positively to society. It breaks the cycle of poverty, promotes gender equality, and fosters economic development.

But the benefits of education extend beyond those who receive it directly. An educated populace is better equipped to make informed decisions, leading to a more vibrant and dynamic community. For the affluent among us, this means a more stable and prosperous environment in which to live and conduct business.

Educated citizens are healthier, more productive, and more engaged in civic activities, creating a ripple effect that enhances the overall quality of life.

By supporting our open sky school, you are not merely making a donation; you are making an investment in the future of our village. Your kindness and generosity will ensure that every child has the chance to reach their full potential, thereby uplifting the entire community.

In closing, I urge you to consider the profound impact your support can have. Let us come together to build a legacy of learning and opportunity. Let us be the catalysts for change and the architects of a brighter tomorrow. With your help, we can transform our village into a place where every child's dream is nurtured under the vast, open sky.

Thank you for your time, your consideration, and your generosity.

Almost everyone in the hall greeted her warmly, praising her eloquence and the amicable manner in which she had conveyed her thoughts. Mukhiya Jee then requested her to wait outside in the veranda until he called for her again. Amid the hum of voices, some muttered, "She should not have been allowed to be among us." Others remarked, "Indeed, if the downtrodden and underprivileged are educated, they would work better in our households and farms." Many concurred, "Education can help them remain clean, and we will not have to keep ourselves away from them." As the murmurs continued, a few affluent members rose and left the hall, but many others stayed, eager to witness the further proceedings of the meeting.

After more than two hours of discussion, Inara Wali was called back into the room. Mukhiya Jee, in a majestic voice, summed up the meeting with the following decisions:

There are seventy affluent families in the village.

Each family will donate 10 rupees every month to Shri Ram Avatar Jee to meet the school's running expenses.

- ➤ The Panchayat will provide two classrooms with furniture.

- ➤ The provision of food for the students and the salary of the teachers will be managed by Mukhiya Jee himself. He also promised to construct three toilets—one for the staff, one for the girls, and one for the boys.

- ➤ Additionally, Inara Wali will teach at the school.

- ➤ The village Panchayat appointed Inara Wali to oversee the Panchayat library every day from 3:00 PM to 5:00 PM, for which she will receive a salary of 100 rupees per month in addition to her school salary.

The announcement was met with loud applause, with everyone hailing Mukhiya Jee for his groundbreaking decisions. These resolutions were seen as a revelation for all present. It was a stroke of luck for Inara Wali, who was likely the first woman from her community to be appointed as a teacher and librarian in a society dominated by men. In those days, it was rare for women to have such roles, if they worked at all, in such a male-dominated environment.

The journey of Inara Wali was far from reaching its end. The path ahead was strewn with challenges she had yet to overcome. Each battle she faced was a step towards earning the social respect she deserved, the equality she sought as a woman, and the rightful status within her community. Though her life remained a relentless struggle, her spirit was unyielding, and her resolve unbreakable. She knew that true conquest lay not in mere victories, but in the unwavering pursuit of justice and recognition.

When Puttalli Gacch, the tree, saw Inara Wali being educated, employed, and looking forward to her next challenges in life, it felt a range of desires and emotions for Inara Wali and her community. Puttalli Gacch admired Inara Wali's achievements and viewed her as a source of inspiration. Seeing someone from her community reaching such heights filled the tree with a sense of pride and hope, motivating it to support others in similar pursuits. The tree anticipated similar progress and success for the entire community. Inara Wali's journey strengthened Puttalli Gacch's resolve to encourage education, employment, and personal growth among all who rested under its shade.

Puttalli Gacch longed to see traditional barriers and social constraints overcome. Inara Wali's success exemplified the benefits of embracing change, and the tree wished to inspire the community to break free from limitations and strive for their dreams. The tree felt a profound sense of pride in Inara Wali's accomplishments. Her success validated the nurturing environment that Puttalli Gacch provided, reinforcing the importance of support and encouragement within the community. Puttalli Gacch aspired to develop or enhance support systems such as educational programs and mentorship opportunities. The tree wished to create a network that would help others follow in Inara Wali's footsteps, ensuring a future of growth and achievement for all.

In essence, Puttalli Gacch's desires and feelings were centred on leveraging Inara Wali's example to inspire, motivate, and facilitate success among the community, fostering a culture of progress and empowerment under its protective branches.

11

She was Twenty – Five

At the age of twenty-five, Inara Wali graced the village with her transient stay, a soul adorned with the delicate brushstrokes of aesthetics, yet shrouded in the veils of ignorance towards her own youthful radiance. Her form bore the weight of neglect, a canvas marred by the strokes of a toxic and dissolute existence.

The melody of her name danced upon the lips of all who dwelt within the village, a siren's call that ignited the hunger within their souls. But beneath the surface of their curiosity lay a darker truth, for she belonged to the different societal status, condemned to the fringes of society's embrace. In the eyes of her peers, she bore the mark of inferiority, a stigma that branded her virtue as currency for the taking. Denied the privilege of prosperity, the inferiors languished in the shadows, their aspirations suffocated by the weight of societal disdain, their very existence tethered to the whims of a prejudiced hierarchy. Within the confines of Malanga, they dared not dream of liberation, for in this realm, freedom was a luxury reserved for those deemed worthy by birthright.

The hamlet, nestled within the comforting embrace of 'tolas,' each a vibrant tapestry woven with the threads of community, she found her dwelling amidst the whispered alleys of the far end enclave. Far away from the stately abode of Mukhiya Jee, the esteemed village patriarch, her modest home stood as a silent witness to the bustling affairs of daily life. Amidst the throngs of eager suitors, both youthful and mature, adorned in their finery, the pursuit of Inara Wali was an endless dance of anticipation. Yet, amidst the joviality that enveloped her doorstep, she harboured a silent discontent, an unwelcome spectre born of the rigid constraints of tradition. For she, in her quiet rebellion against the confines of orthodoxy, found solace in the sanctuary of her faith. With a voice tempered by reticence and eyes alight with unspoken wisdom, she navigated the complexities of existence, offering naught but a gentle smile in the face of life's intricacies.

In the serene theme of village life, Mukhiya Jee remained stoic, untouched by the fleeting gestures of those who mocked and misled the weary souls. Amidst this tableau, Inara Wali emerged as a resplendent figure, adorned with cascading tresses that whispered tales of ancient lore. Her gaze, akin to a wellspring of myriad Legend, spoke volumes, each blink a graceful dance of her eyelashes. Not a hint of strain marred her countenance, for her beauty was a tranquil oasis untouched by the ravages of time. She became the embodiment of allure, the focal point of whispered admiration that rippled through the village like gentle whispers on a breeze. Some found fascination in the silken strands of her hair, while others were enraptured by the delicate curve of her nose, and still, there were those enchanted by the depth of her eyes, their depths unfathomable. As the hands of time continued their unrelenting march, her transition into adulthood bore witness to the passage of seasons, each one a testament to the ephemeral nature of youth's bloom.

In the ethereal fabric of existence, there danced the enigma of Puttali Gacch—a conundrum draped in veils of mystery, a puzzle with no tangible solution. She was a symphony of illusions, a mirage that tantalized the senses, leaving the mind ensnared in a labyrinth of hallucinatory whispers. While some dared to question her corporeality, the collective consciousness surreptitiously painted vivid portraits of her presence, a testament to the bewitching allure she cast upon all who crossed her path.

In the delicate caress of her presence, even her shadow danced gracefully, refraining from earthly embrace. Amidst the vast expanse of societal solitude, she found solace, fashioning it into the very essence of her resilience. She refused to be bound by the constraints of societal norms, her spirit honed and fortified in the crucible of relentless perseverance. In the tapestry of life, youth emerge as the radiant embodiment of boundless hope and unyielding spirit. It is a time when the heart brims with the purest essence of optimism, reaching toward the heavens with unwavering faith. Within the embrace of youth, there exists a profound understanding untouched by the constraints of experience and distinctions between capability and inadequacy dissolve into insignificance. Unbound by the shackles of authority, youth dances to its own rhythm, propelled by an inexorable determination that defies all odds. Fearlessly, it plunges into the depths of uncertainty, a beacon of light amidst the darkness, casting its brilliance to illuminate the path ahead.

With an exuberance that seemed to emanate from the very depths of her being, she embarked upon her noble endeavour. Like a celestial maestro orchestrating a symphony of unity, she birthed a palpable sense of concord among her people. With tireless determination, she laboured to shield not only herself but also her beloved community from the insidious grasp of ignominy and disrepute.

12

Mahesh & Inara Wali

In the rustic state of village life, death, in its solemnity, seemed to possess a humility far surpassing the harsh existence endured by the marginalized communities. Among them dwelled Mahesh, the youngest scion of Mukhiya Jee's second wife, whose soul resonated deeply with the ancient stones of Inara Wali. He stood as a beacon of rebellion, a tempest of societal defiance. Fearlessly, he voiced his truths, heedless of societal norms or individual sensibilities. Mahesh, in his relentless pursuit of justice, tirelessly championed the cause of the marginalized, much to the chagrin of his own kin, who clung to the fragile threads of societal acceptance. Yet, amidst the disapproval, a tender affection blossomed, transforming the initial gestures of polite acknowledgment into an ardent and solicitous romance, echoing the timeless rhythm of love's enduring dance.

Inara Wali savoured the moment, allowing the air to fill her lungs with a delicate grace. In that suspended pause, she discovered a companion with whom to share her deepest desires and fervours. She embarked on a journey of exploration, delving into the marvels of drawn-out breaths - breaths that whispered of unity, harmonious exhales that defied the constraints of hierarchy. In those shared breaths, she found a timeless bond, an emancipation of spirit and flesh intertwined in boundless freedom.

In the early hours, when the sun cast its first golden tendrils upon the waking world, Mahesh emerged as a living tapestry woven from the threads of Gandhi's resilience, Netaji's valour, and Baba Ambedkar's unwavering commitment to justice. To her, he embodied a realm of possibility she had scarcely dared to imagine. With each dawn, she anticipated his presence, a beacon drawing her closer with an irresistible allure. Together, they embarked on a shared odyssey of noble aspirations, their hearts alight with a fervent dedication to the welfare of their fellow beings. Theirs was a mission of enlightenment, extending a benevolent hand to uplift the denizens of the countryside and nurture the tender saplings of future generations. With fervent conviction, they echoed the timeless refrain, "God is singular, and we, the progeny of the same divine essence."

Once again, the verdant foliage of the Puttali Gacch caught the eye of passersby, unfurling in a delicate dance of renewal. In the graceful unfurling of nature's embrace, one cannot escape the tether of inflexibility, a thread woven through the cross-stitch of social status, binding hearts and minds in intricate patterns of belief. In the graceful dance of faith's unyielding devotion, let its rigidity unfurl only to cradle the weary, to shelter the forsaken, to embrace the orphaned, or to weave the sewing of societal serenity. Thus, through steadfast resolve, they reaped the harvest of their benevolence, as the first light of dawn painted the sky with hues of promise and possibility.

In the quiet corridors of her mind, before the dawn of her grand endeavours, she toiled ceaselessly. Her vision, unfurling with threads of compassion, unfettered by the constraints of convention. With each breath, she sculpted dreams into reality, crafting not just an educational sanctuary for the marginalized, but also a haven of healing and a sanctuary of solace. Time, relentless in its passage, had etched lines upon her face, each one a testament to the battles fought and victories won. Yet, her resolve remained unyielding, steadfast in her mission to break the shackles of inferiority that bound her society. Her noble aspirations, like delicate petals unfurling beneath the harsh gaze of monarchy, garnered accolades and honours. Yet, amidst the adulation, she found herself ensnared by the thorns of tradition, hindered by the weight of societal expectations. And yet, she persisted, a beacon of hope in a world cloaked in shadows of prejudice and ignorance.

13

Shrimati Geeta Devi High School – A Royal Decree

Jan Sagar Pond was a vibrant heart of the village, nestled amidst rambling fields and bordered by a quiet kabristan on one side. Along its serene banks, washermen from the dhobi tola had set up their designated wooden planks, spaced meticulously for their daily chore. They arrived with donkeys laden with bundles of clothes, which they washed rigorously with soap, beating and rinsing them in the pond's water.

The pond teemed with life, home to a plethora of fish that attracted avid anglers hoping for a good catch. At dawn, villagers would venture into the nearby fields for their morning routines, cleansing themselves afterward in the pond's cool waters. The surface of Jan Sagar was adorned with an abundance of lotus plants, adding to its picturesque beauty.

Buffaloes and other cattle were frequently brought to the pond, where they drank and bathed, sharing the water with men and women who performed their daily ablutions, seeking purification. The village priest, too, would immerse himself in the pond, conducting his rituals in the sanctity of its waters. For the affluent and elite, the pond offered a place of leisure, where they floated on inflatable tubes, enjoying the tranquil surroundings. Children, with their boundless energy, would swim across the pond, turning it into their playground.

Jan Sagar Pond was more than just a body of water; it was the lifeline of the village, essential for the everyday lives of its people. It belonged to Mukhiya Jee, who primarily used it to irrigate his fields, yet generously allowed the community to benefit from its resources.

Adjacent to this vital pond, the village was seeing the construction of a new 'open sky school'. This emerging educational space boasted two well-furnished classrooms and three toilets, complemented by a vast open area where children could run and play, ensuring a blend of learning and recreation.

In every sense, Jan Sagar Pond was the essence of the village, a place where life, nature, and community seamlessly intertwined.

In the tranquil town nestled amidst the verdant hills, Shri Ardas Mall Bajaj stood as a pillar of prosperity, his affluence woven through the threads of the cloth trade. Yet, within the opulent tapestry of his life, there lay a void, a poignant absence left by the recent departure of his beloved wife, Geeta. Alone, save for the tender companionship of his young son, Shri Bajaj found solace in the labyrinth of memories, each recollection a delicate echo of the time he and Geeta had shared.

As he navigated the warren of his grief, an earnest desire stirred within Shri Bajaj's heart—a yearning to immortalize the essence of his cherished wife, to ensure that her name resonated eternally. Turning to the venerable Mukhiya Jee, the esteemed leader of the community, Shri Bajaj voiced his plea with a humility born of profound love. With attentive ears, Mukhiya Jee received the entreaty, his gaze reflecting a depth of understanding.

With a heavy yet determined heart, Shri Bajaj expressed his fervent wish to transform an existing school into a bastion of knowledge and opportunity, a sanctuary where every child could flourish. Despite possessing the means to fuel this noble endeavours, Shri Bajaj confessed his lack of knowledge in the art of school management and construction. His only request, imbued with unwavering devotion, was that the institution bear the name of his beloved wife, Geeta, immortalizing her spirit for generations to come.

Though Mukhiya Jee's response was tempered with restraint, a quiet acknowledgment permeated his words, acknowledging the gravity of Shri Bajaj's intent. And in a moment of silent exchange, as if bearing witness to the birth of a timeless legacy, Shri Bajaj entrusted Mukhiya Jee with a humble sum of Rs 50000, a symbolic gesture to commence the journey towards realizing his vision.

Despite any reservations that lingered, Shri Bajaj departed, leaving behind not just a monetary contribution, but a legacy woven from the threads of love and remembrance. And in the quiet corridors of the soul, the whispers of Shrimati Geeta Devi High School began to resonate, a tribute to the enduring power of love and the indomitable spirit of generosity.

Under the azure canopy of the sky, Mukhiya Jee, the esteemed leader of the village, extended his gracious invitation to an assembly of luminaries. Gathered beneath the ancient boughs of the village banyan tree, the members of the panchayat, revered teachers, and dignitaries from the government converged to deliberate upon a noble idea. Their purpose: to weave dreams into reality, to breathe life into aspirations.

In the hallowed chambers of discourse, amidst murmurs of anticipation and echoes of reverence, they paid homage to the benevolence of Shri Bajaj. His philanthropy, like a shimmering beacon, illuminated the path of their collective endeavours. They spoke in hushed tones of his unwavering commitment, his unwavering dedication to the betterment of their cherished community.

With hearts brimming with admiration and souls aglow with gratitude, they resolved to honour Shri Bajaj in a manner befitting his magnanimity. Laden with garlands of fragrant blooms, trays adorned with saccharine delights, and blossoms plucked from the gardens of their affection, they embarked upon a pilgrimage to his humble abode.

And there, amidst the countryside charm of his modest shop, Shri Bajaj beheld the procession with misty eyes and a heart overflowing with joy. Tears, like crystalline pearls, traced a path down weathered cheeks as he stood, humbled by the reverence bestowed upon him. In that moment, amidst the warmth of camaraderie and the embrace of community, his spirit soared, finding solace in the beauty of human connection and the power of collective goodwill.

In the inaudible clasp of the village, a flurry of activity stirred the tranquil air as the esteemed Mukhiya Jee, wielding the entirety of the governmental apparatus, orchestrated a symphony of change. With meticulous planning, budgeting, and design, a grand transformation was heralded for the humble village school, whispered by the rhythmic beat of drums traversing its dusty lanes.

Words spread like wildfire through the rustic hamlet as drummers, the heralds of change, proclaimed the imminent metamorphosis: the modest school for the underprivileged would blossom into a bastion of knowledge, expanding its reach to embrace students up to the tenth grade. Under the benevolent gaze of the Nepal Board, its accreditation would bestow upon it a newfound prestige.

But this was not merely a tale of lofty promises; it was a narrative of swift action. With an ambitious timeline of six full moons, the village beheld the promise of a sprawling edifice, rising from the earth like a phoenix from the ashes. Its walls would echo with the laughter of eager learners, its corridors bustling with the rhythm of academic pursuit. And beyond the confines of the village, the drumbeats carried on the wind, beckoning from neighbouring hamlets to partake in the bounty of the Open Sky School—an enterprising venture promising not just education, but opportunity, to all who dared to dream.

Inara Wali and her community were suffused with an overwhelming joy of accomplishment. Among the myriad struggles and hardship, they faced, securing education stood as the paramount milestone. As time marched forward, the school was built with immense enthusiasm, despite the reluctance and disapproval of the affluent residents from surrounding villages. Against all odds, construction and furnishing were completed on schedule, and the school was set to open for the new session.

To spread the word, drummers were dispatched far and wide, informing villagers about the school's inauguration and encouraging them to send their children. Inara Wali, along with her classmates from Open Sky School—Shri Ram Avatar, Shri Govind, Mahesh, and his friends—immersed themselves in tireless public relations work. They strove to build confidence among the poor parents, who had long lived under suppression and were fearful of the unknown implications of this new institution. The affluent villagers, feeling threatened, had already begun to withdraw the meagre facilities they had previously granted out of condescension.

This was more than a mere campaign; it was a battle of ideologies. Support and opposition swelled from many villages, drawing in members of Inara Wali's community, some affluent allies, and numerous educated, independent thinkers. For a fortnight, the region was a scene of revolution. Slogans were chanted, processions marched, and drummers broadcasted the news. People utilized every possible means to propagate their beliefs, both for and against the school. It felt as though the area was on the brink of an election, with the fervour and passion of a populace in the throes of a transformative struggle.

The clamour of revolution resonated far and wide, capturing the attention of daily newspapers that chronicled the unfolding events and impending social changes poised to emerge. These newspapers once again published the photograph of Inara Wali alongside Mukhiya Jee and the teachers, thrusting the matter into the public eye and ultimately reaching the ears of the monarchy.

In response, His Majesty issued a decree, disseminated through the Chief District Officer (CDO) of Malanga, commanding all parties to maintain tranquillity. The royal edict proclaimed that, by His Majesty's will and pleasure, the school would continue to operate as planned. Furthermore, the decree mandated that all necessary government support be provided to facilitate this noble endeavour. His Majesty's order also specified that the school's affiliation with the School Board of Nepal be granted without delay, ensuring the institution's formal recognition and support.

What a moment it was! Joy and happiness filled the air. Meanwhile, Inara Wali, Mukhiya Jee, Shri Bajaj, the teachers, and Mahesh were lauded by the district administration for their exemplary approach and remarkable achievements. However, not everyone shared in the celebration. Many affluent individuals and government officials were displeased with the decision. Though they remained silent, they were determined to obstruct the progress of the school by any means necessary.

Finding qualified teachers proved to be a formidable challenge. The affluent and educated elite, having dismissed the very idea of this endeavour, forbade their men and women from working at the school. From other communities, people lacked the necessary education. Ultimately, teachers were recruited from the neighbouring Indian town of Chandbarsha. Five educators were appointed to teach various subjects in accordance with the Nepal Board curriculum. The school was well-equipped in nearly every respect.

A month later, following a brief prayer ceremony, followed by the garlanding ceremony to the statue of late Shrimati Geeta Devi Bajaj, the school commenced operations with 128 students, five teachers, and three support staff. Mahesh assumed the role of officiating Principal. Shri Ram Avatar and Govind Paswan were designated as the school's directors. Inara Wali was appointed as the mentor for all students hailing from her community. These students came from at least six different villages. Notably, no students from affluent families were enrolled, other than the son of Shri Ardas Mal Bajaj.

At first, the students appeared shabby and unclean; their clothes emitted a foul odour. However, under the diligent mentorship of Inara Wali and with additional sponsorship from the local community, these challenges were soon overcome. A significant milestone had been achieved.

14

Social Justice Conversation At The Panchayat Library

Inara Wali began her new role as the librarian for the Panchayat library with a heart full of hope and a spirit eager to transform. On her first day, she wore a new sari and blouse, her lips adorned with a hint of lipstick. Her hair flowed freely over her shoulders, and a loving smile graced her face. She was the sole staff member in a library that housed around two thousand books, scattered without any index or accession numbers. The racks were grimy, and many books were in a state of disrepair.

Undaunted by the task ahead, Inara Wali chose to start with a thorough cleaning. She organized the books by genre, diligently stamping each one and recording their details in a stock register. She also arranged the furniture to create a welcoming space for readers and set up a register for book loans. Gradually, the library began to take shape, emerging from chaos into order.

Weeks passed, yet not a single visitor crossed the threshold. Inara Wali spent her days reading alone, leaving the library at 5:00 PM each evening. A few students from the open sky school, where Inara Wali had once studied and distinguished herself as a role model, were uncertain whether they were permitted to enter the library. The affluent members of the community, on the other hand, stayed away, their attitudes coloured by the conflicting and partially accepted nature of Inara Wali's persona.

Despite these challenges, Inara Wali continued her work with quiet determination, holding onto the hope that her efforts would eventually draw the community into the world of books she had so lovingly organized.

Those who visited Mahendar Park couldn't help but stare at her with their beguiling eyes. Grown boys and men circled her, driven by their lustful desires, and they would pass lewd comments in her direction. Meanwhile, girls and women from other communities gazed at her with a measure of respect, recognizing that she had attained a status that even the women from affluent families couldn't boast of. In this society, men and women were not accustomed to interacting freely with one another, leading to the library being eerily deserted, devoid of its usual visitors.

Despite her love for reading, Inara Wali found the isolation increasingly difficult to bear. Her companions from Open Sky School began accompanying her to the library daily, waiting outside for her so they could return together. Seeking to break the monotony, Inara Wali started a new practice—she would read inside the library and then come outside to share the stories and the contents of the books she had absorbed. This routine continued for a long time, but eventually, Inara Wali found it unfulfilling and uninspiring.

The following evening, Mahesh arrived at the library, and her heart soared with joy upon seeing him. She warmly welcomed Mahesh, who was visibly excited and overwhelmed by the library's orderly arrangement. With a gracious smile, she recorded his arrival time in the register and invited him to select a book. Mahesh chose a book, yet his gaze repeatedly drifted towards her as he turned the pages. She could sense that his interest lay more in conversing with her than in reading. Suddenly, Mahesh broke the silence, his voice earnest and thoughtful. "What do you think about the importance of social justice in a civilized society?" he asked.

And in the heart of a bustling city - Mahesh, a social activist, and Inara Wali, a philosopher by nature, sit across from each other, tea cups in hand, engaged in a deep conversation about the importance of social justice in a civilized society.

Mahesh had been reflecting deeply on the concept of social justice, troubled by the persistent issues of inequality, discrimination, and lack of access to basic needs. He expressed his concerns to Inara Wali, noting how society seemed to be failing its most vulnerable members. Inara Wali, echoing his sentiments, emphasized that social justice is indeed the bedrock of a civilized society. She referenced the philosopher John Rawls, who proposed the idea of a "veil of ignorance," a thought experiment where individuals design societal principles without knowing their own position in it. This, she explained, would naturally lead to fairer and more just systems, as people would not want to disadvantage themselves.

Mahesh found this perspective compelling and asked how Rawls' principles of justice as fairness could be applied in today's world. Inara Wali acknowledged the significant gap between theory and practice. Rawls had envisioned two main principles: first, that each person has an equal right to the most extensive basic liberties compatible with similar liberties for others, and second, that social and economic inequalities should be arranged to benefit the least advantaged and be attached to positions open to all under conditions of fair equality of opportunity. However, she observed, today's reality starkly contrasts with these ideals, as systemic barriers and institutional biases continue to perpetuate inequality.

Agreeing with her assessment, Mahesh pointed out the troubling racial and gender disparities in society and asked how these issues could be addressed effectively. Inara Wali proposed a multifaceted approach, starting with the recognition and dismantling of institutional structures that perpetuate discrimination. This, she explained, involves policy reforms, education, and a shift in societal attitudes. She drew on the ideas of critical theorists like Michel Foucault, who argued that power is pervasive and comes from everywhere, necessitating the addressing of power dynamics at all levels of society.

Mahesh concurred, noting the crucial role of education in changing societal attitudes. Inara Wali agreed and highlighted the importance of education in shaping perceptions and values from a young age. She referenced Paulo Freire's "Pedagogy of the Oppressed," which emphasizes the need for an educational system that empowers the marginalized and encourages critical thinking. By fostering a curriculum that includes diverse perspectives and teaches empathy, she argued, we can cultivate a generation that values social justice.

The conversation then turned to economic inequality, with Mahesh expressing concern over the widening gap between the rich and the poor. Inara Wali introduced the concept of "capabilities" as proposed by a philosopher, which assesses justice by individuals' capabilities to achieve the kind of lives they have reason to value. This, she explained, means ensuring that everyone has access to education, healthcare, and the means to participate fully in society. She advocated for redistribution policies, fair wages, and social safety nets as essential components in achieving economic justice.

Mahesh pointed out that redistribution policies often face resistance, especially from those who benefit from the status quo. Inara Wali acknowledged this challenge and suggested fostering a culture of solidarity and mutual benefit. People need to understand that a more just society benefits everyone in the long run. She also referenced philosopher Martha Nussbaum's emphasis on public reasoning and democracy in achieving justice. Transparent dialogue and participatory decision-making, she argued, can help build consensus and reduce resistance.

Shifting the focus to a global perspective, Mahesh noted that social justice is not just a local issue but a global one. Inara Wali agreed, describing global justice as a complex challenge. She referenced theories of cosmopolitanism advocated by thinkers like Kwame Anthony Appiah, which suggest that our moral obligations extend beyond national borders. Addressing global inequalities, she argued, requires international cooperation, fair trade practices, and global governance structures that protect human rights.

In conclusion, Mahesh reflected on the necessity of collective effort at all levels—local, national, and global—to achieve social justice. He asked Inara Wali for final thoughts on how individuals can contribute to this cause. Inara Wali responded that individuals can contribute by staying informed, advocating for policies that promote equity, and supporting organizations working towards social justice. It's about embodying the principles of justice in daily life and striving to create a society where everyone has the opportunity to thrive. She reminded him of Martin Luther King Jr.'s words: "Injustice anywhere is a threat to justice everywhere," emphasizing that individual actions, no matter how small, can make a significant difference.

Mahesh thanked Inara Wali for the enlightening conversation, expressing hope that they could all play their part in building a more just and civilized society. He also complimented her on her superior education and understanding. Inara Wali humbly accepted his compliments, noting that through conversations like theirs, they could spark change and inspire others to join the movement for social justice.

The ideological discourse between Mahesh and Inara Wali highlighted the multifaceted nature of social justice and its crucial role in creating a fair and equitable society. By drawing on philosophical theories and practical approaches, they were in a pursuit to explore the challenges and potential solutions in achieving justice for all.

She lost track of time while conversing with Mahesh, so engrossed in their dialogue that she didn't notice her friends had already departed. As dusk settled around her, she found herself alone. A group of men began to follow her, their vulgar comments piercing the evening air. She remained composed, steadfastly continuing on her path, enduring their idiotic remarks. One man ventured close enough to ruffle her hair, a fleeting invasion that made her jerk her head. Despite this, she pressed on, walking briskly until she finally reached the sanctuary of her home, safe and sound.

In the labyrinth of human experience, few shadows loom as persistently and malevolently as those cast by eve teasing and sexual harassment. These insidious forms of gender-based violence carve deep scars into the lives of women, particularly those from impoverished backgrounds, where the fortress of societal support is often weakest.

Eve teasing, a euphemism that belies the gravity of the act, is not merely an adolescent jest but a profound assault on a woman's dignity and autonomy. It is an unsolicited intrusion, a cruel reminder of the pervasive male gaze that objectifies and dehumanizes. For women ensnared in the web of poverty, the stakes are even higher. These women, already marginalized by economic and social inequities, find themselves further alienated by the oppressive acts of those who wield power through intimidation and violence.

Sexual harassment, in its myriad forms, is an affront to the very essence of freedom. It transcends physical boundaries, infiltrating the mental and emotional realms, leaving behind a residue of fear and helplessness. For poor women, this harassment is compounded by a lack of access to justice and support systems. The silence imposed by economic dependency and societal stigma often forces these women to endure in stoic suffering, their voices stifled by the very structures meant to protect them.

In the philosophical expanse, one must contemplate the inherent rights and dignities of human existence. Every woman, regardless of her socioeconomic status, possesses an intrinsic worth that demands recognition and respect. The philosopher's gaze turns to the notions of justice and equity, invoking a moral imperative to dismantle the systems of oppression that perpetuate such violence.

The plight of poor women, subjected to eve teasing and sexual harassment, underscores a profound societal failure. It is a failure to uphold the principles of equality and justice. These women are not mere victims; they are resilient individuals navigating a world fraught with systemic obstacles. Their experiences call upon us to rethink and reshape our societal norms, to foster environments where respect and equality are not privileges but fundamental rights.

To address this scourge, society must engage in a collective introspection. Education and awareness are pivotal, for they sow the seeds of change in the fertile ground of young minds. Legal reforms and stringent enforcement are crucial, ensuring that perpetrators are held accountable and victims are supported. Social support systems must be strengthened to provide safe havens and empower women to speak out without fear of retribution.

In the end, our philosophical journey compels us to acknowledge that the fight against eve teasing and sexual harassment is not just a women's issue; it is a human issue. It demands a collective awakening, a societal metamorphosis where empathy, respect, and justice prevail. Only then can, we hope to create a world where every woman, regardless of her economic status, can walk with her head held high, unburdened by the fear of harassment, and free to pursue her dreams in an environment that celebrates her humanity.

Time moved forward, and one day, a group of elderly women from affluent families graced the library with their presence. It was a heartwarming sight, brimming with joy and aspiration. Inara Wali welcomed them with grace, recording their names and time of arrival, and inquired about the books they were seeking. Some of these women were illiterate, while others had received partial education but struggled with poor eyesight due to their advanced age.

The librarian, eager to assist, asked how she could be of service. The old ladies expressed a heartfelt desire: "We want you to recite verses from the Ramayana for us. If you do that, we will come daily." Given the absence of other visitors, the usual silence of the library seemed unimportant. Inara Wali agreed, and with a respectful ritual of washing her hands, she pulled out the holy Ramayana. She began to recite its verses in a melodious and rhythmic voice, her tone sweet and captivating, drawing the women into a devotional trance.

For an hour, the elderly women were lost in the spiritual cadence of her recitation. As they prepared to leave, each of them offered Inara Wali some money in deep appreciation. Although she initially refused, their insistence prevailed. However, she did not keep the money for herself. Instead, she deposited it into the library's account, meticulously making an entry for each contribution.

This practice continued for over a month. The library, once empty, now buzzed with the presence of these elderly women, who found solace and spiritual nourishment in Inara Wali's recitations. Despite their failing eyesight, their hearts and spirits were alight with devotion.

Inara Wali approached Mukhiya Jee to inform him about the various activities taking place in the library. During their conversation, she mentioned a pressing concern: many elderly women in the village were suffering from severe eyesight problems. Moved by their plight, Mukhiya Jee requested Inara Wali to draft a letter to the Chief District Officer, seeking assistance for a free eye camp to be organized by the government.

The following morning, Inara Wali meticulously composed the letter, which Mukhiya Jee then signed. She personally delivered the letter to the Chief District Officer, who received her with kindness and respect. He assured her that the eye camp would be arranged promptly.

True to his word, a month later, a three-day free eye-checking camp was set up in the Panchayat Library. Mukhiya Jee ensured that word spread throughout the village, encouraging all men and women with vision impairments to attend and receive free treatment.

Recognizing the inclusive spirit of the initiative, Inara Wali approached Mukhiya Jee with a request: to extend the camp's benefits to men and women from other communities as well. Mukhiya Jee agreed, designating the last day of the camp exclusively for individuals from these communities, thereby ensuring that everyone had the opportunity to receive the much-needed eye care.

Thus, through collective effort and compassionate leadership, the village came together to address a vital health concern, fostering a sense of unity and care among all its members.

A palpable excitement and joy swept through the community. Among the gathered were three dedicated doctors, assisted by their helpers, who diligently tended to the villagers' needs. Some patients received soothing eye drops, others were given essential vitamin A tablets, and many were gifted with free spectacles. There was a renewed light in everyone's eyes, and the elderly men and women, donning their new spectacles, exuded a fashionable elegance. Their steps now carried a newfound grace, strength, aspiration, and a profound sense of confidence.

Inara Wali was revered by all, from the elderly of affluent families to members of various communities. Her concern, spirit, virtue, and strength were the subjects of widespread admiration. The villagers regarded her as the most trusted confidante of Mukhiya Jee, bestowing upon her countless unspoken blessings.

The Puttali Gacch, standing tall with its myriad branches, teeming with birds and offering its generous shade to many, symbolized the unwavering strength of Inara Wali. It was under this grand tree that she found her ceaseless inspiration, purpose, and resilience. The Puttali Gacch became a sanctuary of untold ideas, a testament to the enduring spirit of Inara Wali and the lifeblood of the community.

15

Library Battle: Equality Defended

The name and fame of Inara Wali were blossoming exponentially with each passing day. Her ascent, though initially met with resistance, was now compelling even her harshest critics to join her cause, albeit reluctantly. Those who once opposed her found themselves increasingly challenged, their numbers dwindling in the face of her relentless dedication and benevolence.

Bhola Singh and his cohorts were powerless to halt the tide of her growing influence. Every evening, consumed by bitterness and inebriated by liquor, Bhola Singh would rail against Inara Wali, her mentors, and her supporters. His slander spared none involved in the burgeoning wave of progress sweeping through the community. Despite his vociferous opposition, the fruits of social welfare projects were becoming the talk of the town, highlighting the transformative impacts of these initiatives.

Yet Bhola Singh remained steadfast in his resolve. He was determined to uphold the age-old traditions and community systems, convinced that he must thwart any who dared disrupt the status quo.

On a serene afternoon, when the sunlight filtered through the stained - glass windows of the library, he burst in uninvited, his presence shattering the tranquil ambiance. With a tempest brewing in his eyes, he unleashed a torrent of abusive words, each one a sharp shard of malice slicing through the hushed air. His voice, a thunderous symphony of disdain, echoed off the walls, disrupting the serenity that had long held sway.

In his onslaught, he hurled not just insults but also questioned her very essence, her place in society's intricate tapestry of equality. Each accusatory syllable carried the weight of centuries of inequality, as if daring her to defend her right to exist on equal footing with him. And amidst the chaos of his tirade, she stood, a bastion of resilience, her silence a defiant rebuttal to his venomous words.

In that moment, as the clash of his aggression met her unwavering composure, the library transformed into a battleground of ideologies, where the clash between privilege and perseverance played out in the delicate dance of discourse. And though his words may have scorched the air, they could not diminish the quiet strength that emanated from her, a testament to the enduring power of dignity in the face of adversity.

Bhola Singh stood with an air of superiority, addressing Inara Wali with a scornful tone. "Inara Wali, do you even comprehend the nuances of social status?" he sneered. "You, from a lower significance, dare to intrude upon our circle, acting as if you belong."

Inara Wali met his gaze unflinchingly, her voice steady and resolute. "And what makes you believe that your lineage grants you inherent superiority, Bhola Singh? True worth is not bestowed by birth but earned through one's actions and character."

Bhola Singh scoffed, his disdain evident. "Actions and character? Such naïveté! You fail to grasp the power and privilege that accompany noble lineage and esteemed bloodlines."

Her response was calm yet cutting, each word a precise strike. "Your narrow-mindedness betrays you, Bhola Singh. True power is not confined to birthright but resides in deeds and integrity. Our status does not define our worth; our actions and beliefs do."

Incensed by her audacity, Bhola Singh's voice trembled with fury. "Your words reek of insolence! I refuse to engage in discourse with someone who lacks the basic understanding of their place in society."

Inara Wali's expression remained serene; her conviction unwavering. "Perhaps it is you who is blinded by your own arrogance, Bhola Singh. Your refusal to acknowledge the intrinsic value of every individual regardless of caste or status reveals your own shortcomings."

Bhola Singh, unable to refute the undeniable truth in her words, found himself seething in silence. His pride wounded, he stood there, speechless, confronted by the strength of Inara Wali's unwavering belief in the true measure of human worth.

In the bustling heart of the village, amidst the symphony of daily life, a scene unfolded that spoke volumes of resilience, compassion, and the timeless bonds of community. As Bhola Singh's voice echoed through the air, weaving its tendrils of discord, a gathering of venerable women, wise in years and rich in experience, quietly converged, drawn by the currents of empathy and understanding.

They had borne witness to the entirety of the exchange, their keen eyes absorbing every nuance of Inara Wali's ordeal and Bhola Singh's discordant demeanour. With gentle hands and softer words, they enveloped Inara Wali in a cocoon of solace, urging her to disregard the caustic words of one such as Bhola Singh. In their collective wisdom, they reaffirmed her intrinsic worth within the fabric of their society, with the threads of resilience, fortitude, and unwavering resolve.

For Inara Wali, their presence evoked a kaleidoscope of memories – a journey through the labyrinth of childhood innocence, the stark reality of widowhood, and the crucible of toil and sacrifice that had sculpted her into the woman she was today. As the old women departed, their steps weighted with the burden of witnessed sorrow, they carried with them the tale of Inara Wali's tribulation, a narrative of injustice that stirred the hearts of their kinfolk, igniting flames of indignation and solidarity.

And so, as the sun rose anew, casting its golden tendrils over the village, a procession of youth, guided by the matriarchs of their lineage, made their way to the hallowed sanctum of the library. It was a tableau of hope and renewal, a testament to the resilience of the human spirit.

The librarian, a custodian of knowledge and harbinger of enlightenment, extended an offer of comfort, proposing to regale the young minds with the verses of the Ramayana. Yet, in a display of quiet empowerment, one of the elder women gently declined, citing the newfound clarity bestowed by spectacles. Instead, she bestowed upon the children the gift of self-discovery, entrusting them with the sacred task of exploring the epic tales that lay within the pages of their shared sanctuary.

And so, against the backdrop of assumed verses and shared laughter, the library began to unfurl, its threads winding a narrative of hope and possibility. In the clasp of community, the seeds of change took root, blossoming into a sonata of empowerment and enlightenment. Truly, it was a sight to behold – the nascent triumph of a noble endeavour, poised on the cusp of greatness.

16

Love's Eternal Melody

Mahesh sat in the twilight, his back resting against the ancient Puttali Gacch tree. Immersed in the haunting strains of Raag Bihag on his flute, he seemed to merge with the evening's tranquillity. The river Jheem, flowing beside the venerable tree, occasionally splashed cool droplets onto his face. This serene moment, however, belied the river's capricious nature. Whenever rain fell heavily in the upper reaches of Nepal, the Jheem and its tributaries swelled into torrents, flooding the banks, disrupting transportation, and devastating the crops in the fields that flanked its course.

Amid the diminishing day light, and the sound of vividly flowing river water – Mahesh played Raag Bihag undisturbed. As the twilight gently caressed the horizon, the haunting melody of Raag Bihag emanated from the flute, weaving through the tranquil landscape like a sighed prayer. The diminishing light casted a soft, golden hue over the riverbank, where the water swelled with a vivid, almost sentient beauty, its murmur harmonizing with the notes of the flute. The sound of the river, rich and full, mingled with the soulful strains of Raag Bihag, creating a symphony that celebrated the ephemeral beauty of nature. Amidst that unflustered yet vibrant backdrop, his thoughts turned to Inara Wali, his beloved. In that moment of tuneful convergence, he sent her a silent message carried by the music and the whispering waters: that just as the river flowed endlessly, his love for her remained boundless and eternal, a tribute to the beauty that surrounded them and the deeper beauty within their hearts.

As the sun dipped below the horizon further, casting an amber glow over the landscape, Inara Wali made her way home with her cattle. The air was filled with a gentle, soothing melody that seemed to float on the evening breeze. Drawn by the enchanting music, she approached Puttali Gacch and found Mahesh seated beneath the ancient tree, his fingers effortlessly coaxing notes from his flute.

Inara Wali sat quietly beside him; her presence as soft as the twilight. Lost in his music, Mahesh remained unaware of her arrival, his eyes closed in serene concentration. The melody wove emotions around them, binding their souls with invisible filaments.

After some time, Mahesh's eyes opened and met Inara Wali's gaze. The music ceased, but the silence between them was filled with unspoken words. Their eyes locked, conveying a love story as ancient as the stars, a saga of desire and longing that transcended words. The silent conversation between their eyes was profound, speaking of passions and dreams, of an ocean of desires yearning to be fulfilled.

Without touching, without a single embrace, they communicated a deep, boundless love. The subtle movements of their lips, the gentle flicker of their eyelashes, and the graceful gestures of their hands painted a picture of their affection. Each glance, each shared smile, each delicate tilt of the head expressed more than any words ever could.

In that moment, their souls danced together, content and complete in their connection. The absence of physical touch did not diminish their love; rather, it amplified it, making their bond even more sacred. The evening air around them shimmered with the intensity of their unspoken promises, and they found pure contentment in the depth of their silent communion.

As dusk settled over the terrain, Inara Wali left him with a series of gestures, a silent farewell that echoed in the growing darkness. Others, too, were making their way home, guiding their cattle along familiar paths. Inara Wali joined them, her silhouette blending into the group as they moved away. Mahesh remained seated, lost in profound contemplation. His mind churned with thoughts of their love, its potential and perils, and he conversed with himself, pouring out his heart in silent monologue.

He was at a loss for words, unsure how to articulate his feelings to her or to his own family. The prospect of an inter-caste marriage, a rarity in their society, loomed large and threatening. The rigid social norms and the fear of ostracism weighed heavily on him, rendering him mute and petrified. Overwhelmed, he returned home late, his spirit burdened by the unresolved dilemma.

Day by day, Mahesh withdrew further into himself. His appetite waned, his words grew scarce, and a pervasive fear shadowed his every thought. He was constantly seeking a way to marry Inara Wali despite the barriers. Concerned, his colleagues at school, friends in the village, and family members frequently inquired about his health, his silence, and his increasing isolation. They sensed his turmoil, yet the depth of his inner struggle remained unspoken, a silent cry for resolution.

In human relationships, few threads are as complex and profound as those woven through the institution of marriage. In the Indo-Nepal subcontinent, the evolution of this sacred bond has been a testament to both the resilience of tradition and the transformative power of progress. Fifty years ago, the mere notion of an inter-caste marriage was not just an anomaly; it was a defiance of societal norms that reverberated through the very foundations of communities.

Half a century ago, the rigid caste system held an unyielding grip on the structure of society in India and Nepal. Marriages were orchestrated with meticulous attention to caste lines, ensuring the perpetuation of social hierarchies. These unions were seen as essential in preserving the purity of one's lineage and upholding the family's honour. The notion of love transcending these deeply entrenched boundaries was met with staunch resistance, often resulting in social ostracism, familial disownment, and, in extreme cases, violence. The dogmatic views of that era were a reflection of a society deeply rooted in orthodoxy, where deviation from prescribed norms was tantamount to rebellion.

Despite the formidable barriers, the flicker of change was kindled by the spirit of youthful defiance and the gradual but steady spread of education. The winds of modernity brought with them a new consciousness, one that questioned the validity of caste-based discrimination. Yet, the journey was fraught with peril. The courage required to embark on an inter-caste marriage was immense, demanding a willingness to endure societal scorn and the potential for personal peril. Those who dared to love across caste lines became the silent revolutionaries, their unions not merely personal choices but acts of resistance against an oppressive system.

In contrast, today's landscape, though not entirely free from prejudice, has seen significant strides towards acceptance and inclusivity. The sacrifices of those early pioneers have paved the way for a more open-minded generation, one that increasingly values the essence of human connection over the superficiality of caste. The story of inter-caste marriage in the Indo-Nepal subcontinent is thus one of gradual emancipation, where love and progress have slowly but surely chipped away at the edifice of antiquated dogma. It is a poignant reminder that true societal transformation is often born from the courage of those willing to challenge the status quo, one love story at a time.

17
Community Voice Rises

In the open-air school and later at Shri Mati Geeta Devi High School, the boys and girls nurtured under the same sky grew up with a common virtue akin to that of Inara Wali. Enrolled in a superior and well-organized training program, they embarked on their educational journeys, each cultivating their unique perspectives and approaches. Despite preparing for the same school examinations, their interpretations of societal issues, interactions with the opposite sex, and dealings with the affluent varied widely. They confronted societal problems vocally, expressing their convictions passionately, sometimes even responding with force when their dignity or equality was challenged. Yet, they were evolving into well-educated citizens, a fact that satisfied their teachers as they progressed through home examinations.

As the board examinations loomed a month away, the students, now a cohort of 27, were well-prepared. When the results were published two months later in the daily newspaper 'Gorkha Patra', a wave of joy swept through the community: 26 students had passed with first-division, and one with second division. The students and their teachers were celebrated for their remarkable achievements. Shri Ardas Mal Bajaj and Mukhiya Jee honoured everyone with cash prizes, medals, and certificates, recognizing their hard work and dedication.

The reputation of the school had spread far and wide, drawing students from distant communities eager for a quality education. Due to limited resources, the school eventually had to close admissions for the session. Meanwhile, affluent families opted to send their children to a boarding school in a faraway village, rather than enrolling them in their own village's school. Unfortunately, the academic performance at this distant school was consistently poor.

After a couple of years, some of these affluent families sought to enrol their children in the well-regarded village school. However, the Principal maintained a strict policy: admissions were based solely on merit, requiring every prospective student to pass an entrance exam. This policy enraged the affluent families, who felt entitled to bypass such requirements. They pleaded with Mukhiya Jee, questioning how the principal could deny admission to their children. They argued that merit tests should apply only to students from other communities, not to those from their own distinguished backgrounds.

The affluent families further insisted that their children should be segregated into separate classrooms, where they could be educated in a manner befitting their esteemed lineage. Their underlying motive was clear—they sought to establish their supremacy within the school. Mukhiya Jee listened to their grievances with patience and attention, finally assuring them that he would convene a village panchayat meeting soon to deliberate on the matter.

All the children who had completed their grade X examinations found themselves with nothing to do, as there were no facilities for further education in the nearby vicinity. Consequently, they resumed their work on the farms and with the cattle. However, the son of Shri Ardas Mal Bajaj went to Sitamarhi, a nearby town, to continue his education.

In the absence of educational opportunities, these boys and girls became the voice of their voiceless community, advocating against the misery that plagued their lives. The affluent members of society found it increasingly difficult to bully them, pay them less, or demean them. They addressed Inara Wali as "Didi" and supported her unwaveringly in all spheres and on all occasions. For the first time in living memory, the community, partly equipped with education, found its voice and learned to say "no" to injustice.

A week had unfurled its gentle embrace, and the air in the four villages – called Chau Gama hummed with anticipation. Mukhiya Jee's decree, whispered by the winds, had traversed not only the cobblestone paths of their village but had reached the ears of four neighbouring hamlets, weaving unity known simply as Chau Gama – the amalgamation of four distinct realms.

As the sun ascended its throne on that Saturday morn, an opus of diversity unfolded. The affluent denizens, adorned in their opulent attire, mingled with the souls of disparate communities. Dignitaries, with the weight of governance etched upon their brows, found solace in the embrace of wooden chairs, arranged with precision. And amidst this tableau, Mukhiya Jee reigned supreme, his presence an ideal of authority.

Two rows, meticulously formed, delineated the congregation. One, a witness to prosperity, housed the elite; the other, a tapestry of varied hues and backgrounds, spoke of inclusivity and harmony. In this mosaic of humanity, the essence of Chau Gama was palpable – a microcosm where differences melted into a symphony of collective purpose.

In the serene embrace of Chau Gama's communal gathering, two figures emerged from the tapestry of diversity, each bearing the weight of their respective worlds upon their shoulders. Prabhakar, adorned in the regalia of affluence, stood as a sentinel of privilege, while Inara Wali, draped in the cloak of the marginalized, embodied the resilience of the lower community. Their encounter, poised at the intersection of history, philosophy, and human consciousness, unfurled like a saga of epochs past, weaving a narrative that transcended the confines of time.

As the morning sun cast its golden rays upon the assembly, Prabhakar and Inara Wali embarked upon a discourse that echoed the chronicles of civilizations long gone. With each word uttered, they summoned the spirits of empires and revolutions, weaving narratives that spanned the breadth of human existence.

Prabhakar, a scion of affluence, traced the lineage of privilege back through the annals of time, invoking the grandeur of empires past. The spoke of dynasties adorned in gold and marble, where opulence reigned supreme, and the stratification of society was etched in stone. Drawing from the wellspring of history, he painted a portrait of prosperity as the natural order of existence, a divine mandate bestowed upon the chosen few.

Inara Wali, however, emerged as the voice of the downtrodden, channelling the collective suffering and resilience of the lower community. With a heart heavy with the burdens of the marginalized, she invoked the spirits of revolutionaries and visionaries who dared to challenge the status quo. Her rhetoric, infused with the fire of righteousness, echoed the sentiments of philosophers who championed the cause of equality and justice, citing historical precedents of upheaval and transformation.

As the discourse unfolded, the chasm between privilege and adversity widened, echoing the perennial struggle of humanity to reconcile its disparate parts. Fact and fable intertwined, blurring the lines between reality and myth, as Prabhakar and Inara Wali delved into the depths of human consciousness.

The soft murmurs of conversation gave way to a crescendo of impassioned debate, each word a brushstroke on the canvas of societal consciousness. Their discourse, spanning epochs and ideologies, echoed the eternal quest for equilibrium in a world fraught with dichotomies.

As the sun dipped below the horizon, casting long shadows upon the gathering, Prabhakar and Inara Wali stood as emissaries of a new dawn, their discourse a proof to the resilience of the human spirit and the enduring power of dialogue to transcend the barriers of time and space. And in the heart of Chau Gama, amidst the history and the echoes of philosophy, a seed was planted – a seed of change, destined to blossom into a future where unity and understanding would reign supreme.

Yet, amidst the verbal tumult, there lingered a whisper of hope – a collective yearning for a future where the divisions of class and creed would dissolve like mist before the morning sun, giving rise to a society bound by the unbreakable bonds of compassion and empathy.

In the heart of rural tranquillity, under the benevolent gaze of Mukhiya Jee, the anticipation hung thick in the air like the morning mist before dawn. With a solemn decree, he declared that the weighty decisions, like ripened fruits, would be plucked and shared amongst the eager populace the following day, bidding all to return to their dwellings. Across the verdant expanse, from the humble tea stalls to the bustling market squares, and within the intimate confines of households and gatherings, there echoed a symphony of voices, each eager to contribute to the discourse.

It was not merely a conversation; it was a fervent battle for the sacred ideals of education - a battle that transcended the boundaries of caste, creed, and status. Men, women, and children alike stood united in their yearning for equitable opportunities, their hearts beating as one in the rhythm of solidarity. And thus, with bated breath, they awaited the verdict of the Village Panchayat, their hopes buoyed by the promise of a brighter tomorrow.

Gathered in solemn council, Mukhiya Jee, accompanied by the esteemed headmen of neighbouring villages, dignitaries, and the venerable Shri Bajaj, engaged in impassioned deliberation with the custodians of knowledge - the revered school teachers. After much contemplation and discourse, Mukhiya Jee unveiled his decision like a cherished treasure, one that would shape the destiny of generations to come.

The verdict was clear yet laden with responsibility: the school, like a flare of enlightenment, lacked the capacity to accommodate the burgeoning tide of eager minds. Each member of the community was called upon to contribute to the expansion of the school, to erect new classrooms, a mess hall, and dormitories, and to provide for the recruitment of additional teaching and non-teaching staff.

Yet, amidst the weight of obligation, there shimmered a ray of altruism. Shri Ardas Mal Bajaj, with a spirit as generous as the open sky, extended his benevolent hand, offering to shoulder the burden of provision. But his offer came with a condition, a solemn vow to uphold the sacred principles of equality - to erase the lines of caste, gender, creed, and status, and to ensure that every child, regardless of background, would find sanctuary within the hallowed halls of learning.

The echoes of Mukhiya Jee's proclamation reverberated through the village, casting a spell of anticipation over the land. For nine days, the silence of contemplation enveloped the community, until finally, like petals unfurling to the sun's gentle caress, the dignitaries and the affluent emerged, their hearts aligned with the noble cause.

With solemn resolve, they approached Mukhiya Jee, their signatures etching a covenant of unity and purpose. And thus, with ink-stained parchment in hand, they forged a pact with destiny, binding themselves to the sacred tenets of the school's ethos. And so it came to pass, amidst the whispers of wind passing through the Puttali Gacch and the songs of birds in flight, the school blossomed into a sanctuary of enlightenment, a haven where the pursuit of knowledge knew no bounds. Through the corridors of time, it stood as an acknowledgement to the power of community, carrying the hopes and dreams of countless alumni upon its sturdy shoulders.

In the human existence, education stands as the cornerstone of empowerment, transcending the boundaries of gender, caste, creed, and societal status. It is the sign of hope that illuminates the path of every individual, irrespective of their background, guiding them towards the realms of knowledge and enlightenment.

In a world where prejudice and discrimination often cast their shadows upon the corridors of learning, the pursuit of equal opportunities in education emerges as a verification to the resilience of the human spirit. It is a proclamation of equality, a declaration that every mind, regardless of its vessel, deserves the nourishment of wisdom and the embrace of education.

Gender, once wielded as a barrier to enlightenment, now finds itself dismantled by the relentless march of progress.

No longer shackled by the chains of antiquated norms, women stand tall as guardians of knowledge, their intellect shining brightly in the hallowed halls of academia. With each stroke of the pen and each turn of the page, they rewrite the narrative of history, weaving their stories into the very fabric of human consciousness.

Similarly, the spectre of caste and creed, once used to divide and conquer, now withers in the face of inclusivity and acceptance. The classroom becomes a sanctuary where diversity is celebrated, where every voice, regardless of its accent or origin, resonates with the melody of learning. Here, students from all walks of life come together in a symphony of ideas, each note harmonizing with the next to create a masterpiece of understanding and empathy.

And as for societal status, once seen as a determinant of one's educational destiny, it now bows before the altar of meritocracy. No longer do the gates of knowledge remain barred to those without privilege or pedigree. Instead, they swing wide open, welcoming all who dare to dream, all who dare to aspire, into the embrace of opportunity.

Yet, amidst this melody of progress, let us not forget the journey that still lies ahead. For while strides have been made, there are still those whose footsteps falter on the path to education, still those whose voices are drowned out by the cacophony of inequality. It is our solemn duty, as stewards of enlightenment, to ensure that the flame of equal opportunity continues to burn bright, illuminating the way for generations yet to come.

18

Unity Vs Division

Bhola Singh was seething with rage. His once-unquestioned popularity among the affluent villagers, who resented the evolving social order, was now under threat. These individuals, discontented with the shifting dynamics, despised the erosion of their traditional status. They had reluctantly come to realize that they could no longer exploit the labourers as before, paying them paltry wages, deceitfully mortgaging their lands, and eventually claiming ownership.

The labourers, once submissive, had begun to assert their rights. They demanded fair wages and better meals for lunch, insisted on having water available in the fields, and called for clearly defined working hours with adequate breaks. Their demands extended to compensation for injuries sustained while working, including incidents like snake bites. No longer did they tolerate the abusive language from their masters, retaliating instead with newfound courage.

The situation escalated further as some labourers chose to abandon their oppressive masters, never to return. In a desperate bid to maintain control, the landowners attempted to hire labourers from neighbouring villages, only to be met with refusal in a show of solidarity among the workers. The winds of change were unmistakable, and Bhola Singh's fury reflected the fear and frustration of a class struggling to come to terms with a new reality.

The age-old custom of demeaning the poor and stripping them of their fundamental rights was steadily becoming a relic of the past in the village. With each passing year, more boys and girls emerged from the village school, their numbers bolstering the community's strength and unifying its voice. Within the school's walls, students from every walk of life studied side by side, shared their games, laughter, meals, and dreams. The bonds they formed in this shared space made it impossible to enforce separation in the world beyond the school gates. Gradually, the entrenched divisions between the affluent and the deprived began to crumble.

At Mahendar Park, there was no distinction between boys and girls. They played together under the same sky, their cheers and laughter mingling freely. The rigid, traditional family structures of the affluent were being challenged, their very foundations shaking. Whether met with approval or resistance, the winds of change swept through the village, irrevocably transforming its people and their way of life.

Bhola Singh, a man steadfast in his traditionalism, quietly conspired with the affluent families who supported him. He urged them to stop giving water from their wells and tubewells to those who dared to defy the old ways. He persuaded certain shopkeepers to cease selling groceries to these families, aiming to plunge their lives into deeper misery. Desperation spread as people approached Inara

Wali, lamenting the lack of water for cooking and the refusal of shopkeepers to sell them provisions.

Inara Wali, a woman of formidable resolve, listened to their pleas and declared a bold stance. She announced that those who denied water or groceries would no longer benefit from their labour. Together, they shared what little water and food they had among themselves, deciding unanimously to cease working for any affluent families in the village.

Soon, a crisis engulfed the village. Maids, farm labourers, shop attendants, and sanitary workers all halted their services. The village was thrown into disarray, a cacophony of distress and discontent echoing through its streets. The affluent families, once so secure in their dominance, now faced the formidable force of a united community challenging the old order.

Eventually, the affluent members of the community came to realize that the dire situation had been exacerbated by the actions of certain shopkeepers and some among their own ranks. However, those among the wealthy who possessed kind hearts and rejected such dogmatic views extended a compassionate hand. They invited the affected individuals to draw water from their tube wells and to take groceries from their stores. These workers, though they returned to their labours, resolutely avoided those who had previously spurned them.

Inara Wali, having saved some money by this time, decided to make a lasting contribution to her community. Understanding the importance of accessible water, she invested in a tube well, which cost 500 Rs at the time. She ensured, it was installed in a convenient location at her home, where all her neighbours could come to fetch water, thus providing a vital resource and fostering a spirit of unity and support among them.

The incident spread like wildfire, and soon reached the ears of Mukhiya Jee. Recognizing the gravity of the situation, he summoned both Bhola Singh and Inara Wali to his office. Accompanied by their ardent supporters, the two arrived, each exuding agitation and a readiness for violent confrontation. Mukhiya Jee, with a calm yet authoritative demeanour, requested each of them to recount the events that had transpired. One by one, they began to explain, their voices tinged with anger and tension, as they sought to present their side of the story to the discerning Mukhiya Jee.

In the dimly lit office of Mukhiya Jee, the air was thick with tension and the murmur of voices outside hinted at a community on the brink. Bhola Singh, with his imposing frame and stern expression, stood facing Inara Wali, who, despite the hardship etched into her features, radiated a resolute calm. They were flanked by their supporters, each side bearing witness to a confrontation that had been brewing for days.

Bhola Singh broke the silence first, his voice deep and commanding. "Inara Wali, your community must understand the consequences of defiance. By refusing to adhere to our terms, you only bring suffering upon yourselves. The affluents have already shut off the water supply, and the shopkeepers, at my behest, have agreed not to sell groceries to your people."

Inara Wali's eyes, dark and unwavering, met his. "Bhola Singh," she replied, her voice steady and clear, "it is not defiance but dignity we seek. You may have the power to deny us water and food, but we have the strength of our labour. As long as my community works in your fields, attends to your shops, and cleans your streets, we hold leverage. From this moment, we withdraw our services."

A murmur of shock rippled through the room. Mukhiya Jee, seated behind an ornate desk, raised a hand to silence the gathering. His face, lined with the weight of leadership, bore a look of concern. "This cannot continue," he said, his tone a blend of authority and pleading. "We are one community, and such division will lead to ruin for all."

Bhola Singh's eyes flashed with anger. "Mukhiya Jee, it is they who have caused this rift. They must understand their place and the natural order of things."

Inara Wali's lips curled into a slight, defiant smile. "The natural order you speak of is one of oppression. We will not be subjugated. Our work gives your affluence meaning. Without us, your fields will wither, your shops will stand unattended, and your streets will drown in filth."

Mukhiya Jee leaned forward, his eyes pleading. "There must be a way to resolve this without such drastic measures. Bhola Singh, surely there is a compromise we can reach."

Bhola Singh's voice was a low growl. "Compromise? With them? They must be shown their place."

Inara Wali stepped forward, her presence commanding attention. "Our place, Bhola Singh, is beside you, not beneath you. We are the hands that toil and the backs that bend. Without us, your wealth is meaningless."

The room fell silent, the gravity of her words sinking in. The assembled leaders and community members shifted uneasily, sensing the truth in her statement. Mukhiya Jee sighed deeply, rubbing his temples as he considered the impasse.

"Inara Wali," he began softly, "what do you propose as a path forward? How can we bridge this chasm that threatens to tear our community apart?"

She took a breath, her gaze steady on Mukhiya Jee. "We seek respect and fair treatment. Access to water and food are basic human rights, not privileges to be bestowed or withheld. In return, we offer our labour willingly, but with dignity."

Bhola Singh scoffed. "Dignity? You speak of dignity as if it is yours to demand."

"It is ours to claim," Inara Wali responded fiercely. "We will not be treated as less than human. We will not be starved into submission."

Mukhiya Jee stood, his face stern but compassionate. "Enough," he said firmly. "This stalemate helps no one. Bhola Singh, you must see reason. The strength of our community lies in its unity. We cannot thrive on division and discord."

Bhola Singh's jaw tightened, but he remained silent, glaring at Inara Wali. She, in turn, stood tall and resolute, her quiet strength a stark contrast to his bluster.

Mukhiya Jee continued, "I propose a council be formed, with representatives from both sides, to address grievances and find equitable solutions. Water and food will be restored to Inara Wali's community immediately, and in return, they will resume their work. But this council must ensure that their rights and dignity are upheld."

There was a murmur of approval from the assembled crowd. Bhola Singh's eyes flickered with a mix of anger and reluctant acceptance. "Very well," he said through gritted teeth. "But mark my words, this is far from over."

Inara Wali nodded, a glimmer of triumph in her eyes. "It is just the beginning. A beginning of mutual respect and cooperation."

As they left Mukhiya Jee's office, the tension in the air began to dissipate, replaced by a cautious hope. The path ahead was uncertain, fraught with challenges, but the seeds of change had been sown. The community, once divided, now had a chance to heal and grow stronger together. And in the heart of it all stood Inara Wali, a paradigm of resilience and courage, leading her people toward a future where their dignity would be recognized and respected.

One month later, Mukhiya Jee brought forth news that would forever change the fabric of the village: the installation of several tubewells, accessible to all members of the community. This decision came after a significant discovery: most of the existing wells, claimed by the affluent as their own, were actually dug on government land. These wells, along with temples and dispensaries similarly erected on public property, were now officially declared public facilities. The decision promised to turn these resources into communal assets where everyone could fetch water, irrespective of their social standing.

The Chief District Officer, accompanied by police officials, arrived in the village to oversee the transition. They erected government signboards on all such facilities, symbolizing their new status as public property. Addressing the villagers, the CDO emphasized that times were changing. He underscored the importance of unity and collective effort for development. He sternly warned that any disruptions to the village's peace would be met with the full force of the law.

The response from the village was overwhelmingly positive. Most of the villagers rejoiced at the turn of events, seeing it as a step toward a more inclusive and prosperous future. The air was thick with celebration, and the atmosphere electric with joy. Mukhiya Jee led the festivities, decorating the newly designated public facilities and organizing a grand ceremony. These places were adorned with garlands, and rituals were performed to sanctify them. Sweets were generously distributed, and the sound of laughter and song filled the air.

As night fell, the village's elders and the old-timers indulged in liquor, their spirits lifted high as they joined the chorus of song and dance that lasted till dawn. The sense of communal joy was palpable, a proof to the village's enduring spirit and unity.

Indeed, Puttali Gacch was a picture of happiness and prosperity. This age-old settlement, with its roots deep in history, had always stood as a silent witness to the lives of its inhabitants. It had wished for nothing but their well-being and had prayed for their prosperity. Now, as the village embraced a new era of equality and shared resources, Puttali Gacch seemed to hum with contentment, reflecting the joy and unity of its people.

The celebration continued with unbridled enthusiasm. Men, women, and children danced around bonfires, their shadows flickering against the walls of the village huts. The melodies of folk songs reverberated through the air, accompanied by the rhythmic beat of drums. The night sky, dotted with stars, seemed to watch over the revelry, a silent witness to the village's newfound solidarity.

As the night wore on, stories were exchanged around the fires. Tales of old, of times when the village was divided by invisible lines of wealth and caste, were told and retold. But now, those lines were beginning to blur. The installation of the tubewells symbolized more than just access to water; it was a step towards breaking down barriers and fostering a sense of collective ownership and responsibility.

Mukhiya Jee's leadership was lauded by all. His vision and determination had brought about this change, and the villagers recognized his efforts with deep gratitude. They saw in him a hope, a leader who not only understood the needs of his people but also took concrete steps to address them.

The celebrations marked a turning point for Puttali Gacch. The village, which had seen its share of hardships and struggles, was now on a path of progress and unity. The communal facilities, once symbols of division, were now emblems of unity and shared purpose. The village's collective spirit had been reignited, and there was a renewed sense of hope for the future.

In the glow of the bonfires and under the watchful eyes of the elders, the village danced into the night, celebrating not just the installation of tubewells, but the dawn of a new era. An era where everyone, regardless of their background, could draw water from the same well and where the prosperity of one was the prosperity of all.

Indeed, Puttali Gacch was happy. It had stood through the ages, seen many changes, and now, it witnessed the blossoming of a new beginning. It prayed for the continued prosperity and well-being of its people, its heart swelling with pride and hope. The village was not just a collection of huts and fields; it was a living, breathing entity, vibrant with the life and dreams of its people. And on this night, it celebrated with them, basking in their joy and sharing in their triumph.

Equality of human consciousness and rights, are imperative to delve deeper into the profound essence of parity beyond mere access to resources such as water. While the magnanimous act of Mukhiya Jee in permitting villagers to fetch water from newly installed tubewells and public wells is laudable, it is but a single facet of a much larger arena of human equality.

Historically, the struggle for equality has been a bedrock of human evolution, intricately plaited through the annals of time. From the egalitarian principles espoused by the philosophers of Ancient Greece to the revolutionary cries of "Liberté, égalité, fraternité" during the French Revolution, the quest for equality transcends mere access to tangible resources. It encompasses the profound recognition of the intrinsic worth and dignity of every individual.

The great Mahatma Gandhi once posited that "the true measure of any society can be found in how it treats its most vulnerable members." This axiom accentuates the need for a deeper understanding and practice of equality, one that transcends the physical and touches the very spirit of human coexistence. It is not enough to provide water if the underlying structures of power and privilege remain unchallenged and intact. True equality demands a holistic approach that addresses the socio-economic and cultural barriers that perpetuate inequality.

Philosophically, the notion of equality is deeply rooted in the concept of 'Ahimsa' (non-violence) and 'Satyagraha' (truth force) that Gandhi championed. These principles advocate for a form of equality that is all-encompassing, advocating for social justice, economic fairness, and political inclusion. It calls for an awakening of the collective consciousness to recognize and dismantle the systemic inequities that hinder true equality.

Furthermore, the Universal Declaration of Human Rights, adopted in 1948, articulates the inherent dignity and the equal and inalienable rights of all members of the human family as the foundation of freedom, justice, and peace in the world. This declaration is evidence to the global recognition that equality is not merely about providing resources but about ensuring that every individual has the opportunity to live a life of dignity, free from discrimination and oppression.

In conclusion, while the act of providing free access to water through tubewells and public wells is a commendable step towards addressing immediate needs, it should not be misconstrued as the zenith of equality. True equality requires a continuous and deliberate effort to cultivate a society where every individual is afforded the same rights, opportunities, and respect. It is about nurturing a human consciousness that recognizes and celebrates our shared humanity, and tirelessly works towards the realization of a world where equality is not just a principle, but a lived reality for all.

19

A Big Operation Unfolds

In the calm society of Inara Wali, an unsettling shadow fell upon a humble home. Three young girls had vanished, leaving their parents in a state of frantic despair. Their search began within the village, spreading out to the nearby jungle and the riverbank, but no trace of the children was found. Their hearts heavy with worry, they reached out to relatives in distant villages, hoping for any sign or clue.

Despite their relentless efforts, the parents found no answers. Desperation led them to confide in their neighbours, but this too yielded no results. The community, moved by their plight, gathered to offer solace and strength. Murmurs of possible fates whispered through the air—perhaps the girls had drowned in the river, lost their way in the dense forest, or fallen prey to the wild creatures lurking within.

Inara Wali, upon hearing this heart-wrenching news, took swift action. She approached Mukhiya Jee, the respected leader of the community, to seek his intervention. Mukhiya Jee immediately summoned Mahesh, the local school principal, inquiring if the missing girls were his students. Mahesh confirmed they were, indeed, in class

VI. A stern reprimand followed—how could he have remained unaware and inactive for so long?

Mahesh, deeply remorseful, stood silent as Mukhiya Jee directed them to report the incident to the authorities. Together, they accompanied the grieving parents to the police station, where they lodged a formal missing complaint. The police officer, though initially frustrated by the delay, assured the distraught family that every effort would be made to bring their children back home.

Thus, the community of Inara Wali united in a collective hope, their hearts and prayers focused on the safe return of the three missing girls.

Many months had passed, and the mystery of the missing children lingered like a ghost story told in whispers around the village fires. The police had come up empty-handed, their investigations yielding no clues, and the villagers, weary of their own futile searches, had reluctantly resumed their daily routines. Time, with its relentless forward march, had dulled the collective memory of the community. The once sharp pain of loss had softened into a muted ache, a background sorrow barely acknowledged in the bustle of life. The children, whose laughter once echoed through the streets, had become faint, almost forgotten echoes themselves.

But as spring began to bloom, breathing life back into the fields and forests, the nightmare returned. It was a day like any other when a 12-year-old boy named Raghu vanished. He had been on his way home from school when a shadow fell across his path. A man appeared, sinister and swift, blindfolding Raghu and spiriting him away on a motorcycle. The village, still tender from past losses, was thrust once more into the grip of terror.

Raghu was taken deep into the forest, to a secluded place where the air was thick with the scent of pine and the whisper of unseen creatures. It was there, in a hidden den of despair, that he found the three missing girls. Their eyes, once bright with hope and innocence, now mirrored the darkness of their captivity. Despite the shadows that haunted them, a spark of recognition and a flicker of solidarity ignited as they welcomed Raghu into their midst. They were bound by their shared ordeal, a small, resilient group clinging to each other in the face of their abduction.

Back in the village, the absence of Raghu did not go unnoticed. Mahesh, a principal with a heart attuned to the rhythms of his students, sensed something was amiss. When Raghu failed to appear at school, a gnawing worry took root in his heart. He wasted no time, setting off to visit Raghu's parents. Their home, usually filled with the warmth of familial love, was now a place of sorrow. As Mahesh gently inquired about Raghu's whereabouts, the facade of composure crumbled. His parents, hearts heavy with fear and despair, burst into tears, their grief a raw and aching wound.

Mahesh, ever the compassionate soul, stayed with them, offering words of comfort and solace. He knew that words alone could not bridge the chasm of their pain, but his presence was a small balm to their wounded spirits. After ensuring they were as comforted as they could be under the circumstances, he returned to the heart of the village, his mind racing with the implications of another missing child.

Meanwhile, Mukhiya Jee, the village head, took decisive action. He approached the police officers himself, his demeanour one of quiet determination. The gravity of the situation was not lost on him, nor on the officers who listened to his plea. Mukhiya Jee urged them to act swiftly, to pour their resources into finding the lost children and bringing them home. His voice, usually calm and composed, carried an edge of urgency and desperation. He also requested enhanced security measures, particularly night patrols around the village, to safeguard against further abductions.

The police, galvanized by Mukhiya Jee's impassioned plea, promised to redouble their efforts. They began organizing search parties and planning night patrols, their determination renewed. The village, too, rallied together, their earlier complacency replaced by a fierce resolve. They could not afford to forget again; the children, the heart of their community, had to be found and brought back.

As the sun dipped below the horizon, casting far-seeing shadows across the village, a renewed sense of vigilance and hope took root. The villagers, though gripped by fear, stood united. The forest, once a place of solace and mystery, had become a looming presence, its depths hiding the secrets of their lost children. But within that darkness, there was a flicker of hope. For the children who were almost forgotten were remembered again, and the community, galvanized by their loss, would not rest until they were safe.

When Mukhiya Jee returned from his journey, he was met with a sight both daunting and demanding. Inara Wali, the resolute leader, stood amidst her community members, their faces a blend of worry and hope. As one, they implored Mukhiya Jee to aid them in locating their missing children and to devise a permanent solution to their plight. The air was thick with desperation, a tangible force pressing in on him.

A contingent of four men, their expressions a mixture of determination and desperation, stepped forward. They pleaded with Mukhiya Jee, offering to forgo all the benefits they received if only he would help them find their children. Their voices rose in agitation, turning accusatory as they directed their anger toward Inara Wali. They shouted that since she had assumed leadership, misfortune had plagued them. The scene grew chaotic, voices intertwining in a dissonance of distress and blame.

Mukhiya Jee, with the bearing of a man used to command, surveyed the turbulent crowd. With a stern gaze and a gesture for calm, he silenced the throng. His voice, firm and reassuring, cut through the noise, instructing them to return to their homes peacefully. He assured them that a solution would soon be found.

As the crowd dispersed, their murmurs fading into the distance, Mukhiya Jee allowed himself a moment of respite. He sank into his chair, the weight of his responsibilities settling heavily upon him. Lighting a cigar, he indulged in a brief moment of reflection. His past as a distinguished judge and a celebrated lawyer had bestowed upon him a reputation of unmatched brilliance. His connections reached the highest echelons, extending directly to His Majesty. Mukhiya Jee's influence was formidable, his voice carrying weight in the corridors of power.

As the fragrant smoke curled around him, a thought struck Mukhiya Jee with unsettling clarity. It had been an unusually long time since Bhola Singh, the village's notorious troublemaker, had caused any disturbances. Bhola Singh, whose name was once synonymous with unrest, had not been the subject of any complaints for months. This unusual quietness gnawed at Mukhiya Jee's instincts, raising suspicions that refused to be ignored.

Equipped with a telephone that required the tedious process of dialling through an exchange, Mukhiya Jee began the task of contacting the police. His fingers paused midway, a realization dawning upon him. To maintain the secrecy of his concerns, he gently replaced the receiver. Instead, he chose a more direct approach, setting out for the police station that very afternoon.

Upon his arrival, Mukhiya Jee was greeted by the officer in charge, who listened intently as he shared his apprehensions regarding Bhola Singh. The officer's eyes gleamed with interest, pleased to have a lead in these uncertain times. Immediately, a plan was set into motion. Four officers from the local intelligence unit, clad in civilian attire, were assigned to survey Bhola Singh discreetly. Their mission was clear: to monitor his activities closely and report back daily.

With these measures in place, Mukhiya Jee felt a semblance of relief. Yet, the weight of his duties lingered, a constant reminder of the responsibilities that came with his esteemed position. As he walked back from the police station, the sun dipping low on the horizon, Mukhiya Jee's mind remained occupied with the puzzle of his village's recent troubles. His steps echoed with a resolve to uncover the truth and restore peace to his beloved community.

The police officers, recognizing the gravity of the situation, promptly alerted the forest guards as well as police forces stationed in the neighbouring villages. This set-in motion a painstaking search through the labyrinthine expanse of the jungle, a search made all the more arduous by the relentless pursuit of a shadowy figure known as Bhola Singh. Their efforts revealed a curious pattern: Bhola Singh would venture into the jungle daily, always empty-handed and at varying times. Hours later, he would emerge, laden with bundles and packets, the contents of which piqued the interest and concern of the authorities.

To bolster their efforts, more policemen in civilian attire were summoned. As they explored deeper into the dense foliage, they stumbled upon an astonishing sight—hidden within the heart of the jungle were numerous hollow trees and inconspicuous bamboo huts, skilfully camouflaged with leaves and creepers to evade detection by passersby or forest officers.

The jungle, a realm teeming with life, was anything but silent. The air was frequently pierced by the growls of bears, the roars of lions, and the myriad sounds of other wild creatures. It was also a domain of peril, harbouring some of the deadliest and most venomous snakes known to man.

In this remote and secretive enclave, the police discovered a small community—a group of about five men, six women, and seventeen children of varying ages. These individuals resided within the hollow trunks and bamboo huts, their lives shrouded in secrecy and hardship. The elder members of this group had been entrenched in the grisly business of poaching, driven by their inability to repay the crippling debts they owed to Bhola Singh. Their servitude had been long and unrelenting.

The children, on the other hand, had not chosen this life. They had been abducted, torn from their homes, and made captives in this wilderness. Bhola Singh, in a bid to erase their pasts and obliterate their identities, had renamed them all. This sinister act of renaming was part of his broader strategy to conceal the true nature of his operations.

The huts, though appearing rudimentary, held a grim arsenal. Sufficient arms and ammunition were found stored within, an indication to the underlying danger and preparedness of this clandestine group. Guarding the perimeter were trained sentinels, armed with guns and kukris (Nepalese knife), ensuring that any intruders would face swift and severe repercussions.

Integral to the investigation were the forest officers, whose expertise and intimate knowledge of the jungle proved invaluable. They played a pioneering role, providing critical information that helped piece together the full extent of Bhola Singh's operation. Among their findings were the remains of numerous wild animals, a stark indicator of the poaching activities that had plagued this area for years.

The elders, despite their years of labour, found themselves unable to extricate from the clutches of their debt to Bhola Singh. Meanwhile, the younger captives, bereft of freedom and identity, toiled under his dominion. This bleak existence, hidden from the eyes of the world, featured the ruthless exploitation that Bhola Singh orchestrated within the depths of the jungle.

Thus, the police and forest officers, armed with newfound resolve and vital information, prepared to dismantle the nefarious network that Bhola Singh had meticulously crafted. This operation, steeped in danger and complexity, would require all their skill and determination to bring justice to those oppressed and to restore a semblance of peace to the beleaguered jungle.

Bhola Singh's operation was colossal, deeply entrenched in the heart of the jungle where he coordinated the trade of animal skins and parts. By day, the dense forest seemed serene, a haven where the villagers of Nepal lived in harmony with nature. They revered the forest, relying on its bounty for their daily needs. Firewood to warm their homes, medicinal herbs for healing, timber to build their shelters, nuts and fruits for sustenance, and fodder for their livestock were all provided by the generous forest. This symbiotic relationship had endured for generations, untouched by the taint of greed or violence.

However, beneath this peaceful veneer lurked the shadowy dealings of Bhola Singh. The villagers, simple and honest, could hardly fathom that someone would slaughter the very animals they coexisted with to earn illicit wealth. The thought that their tranquil woods could be the backdrop for such atrocities was unimaginable.

Yet, Bhola Singh did more than just poach animals. He was rumoured to abduct children and keep debtors in perpetual bondage, adding a sinister dimension to his already heinous acts.

One fateful night, the tranquillity of the village was shattered. The authorities, having gathered intelligence about Bhola Singh's despicable activities, decided to act decisively. More policemen were dispatched, and the once quiet village began to resemble a military encampment. The sheer number of police officers bewildered the villagers, who had never seen such a formidable presence in their midst. Fear rippled through the community, the uncertainty of the unfolding events weighing heavily on their hearts.

Under the cover of darkness, Bhola Singh was apprehended. The operation was conducted with utmost secrecy; he was taken from his home silently, spirited away to an undisclosed location. As dawn approached, the police surrounded the poaching site deep within the forest. A fierce battle ensued between the law enforcement officers and Bhola Singh's guards. The crack of gunfire echoed through the trees, disturbing the predawn stillness. After an intense struggle, the police gained control of the area.

The search of Bhola Singh's residence had already yielded a shocking discovery. Hidden beneath his bed, inside furniture, and even within kitchenware, the police found a vast sum of money. This illicit fortune was only a part of the haul. The true horror lay in the stacks of animal parts uncovered: countless deer skins, horns of sambar, snake skins, and even several tiger skins. These grim trophies painted a vivid picture of the scale of poaching Bhola Singh had engaged in.

Deeper in the jungle, the police found the main consignment of animal carcasses and parts. Horns, tusks, skins – the remnants of countless majestic creatures – were piled high, evidence of the rampant slaughter that had taken place. Among these grim finds were also the children, men, and women who had been held captive. The children, their faces etched with fear and confusion, were immediately taken for medical checkups and brief interrogations before being joyfully reunited with their parents. The men and women, victims of Bhola Singh's cruel enterprise, were arrested and taken into custody to ensure their involvement was thoroughly investigated.

The villagers watched in a mix of relief and sorrow as the police rounded up those involved and brought the nightmare to an end. The forest, once a symbol of their peaceful existence, had been tainted by the greed and cruelty of a few. Yet, with Bhola Singh's capture and the rescue of the captives, a sense of justice and hope began to bloom anew in their hearts. The villagers hoped that their beloved forest would once again become a sanctuary, free from the shadows of exploitation and fear.

Inara Wali, Mahesh, and Prabhakar, adorned with garlands, gathered together and showered praise upon Mukhiya Jee for his resounding victory. A serene calm settled over the village, as the air buzzed with conversations about the infamous deeds of Bhola Singh. His family was cloaked in deep shame; they avoided the village folk, who in turn shunned them completely. Bhola

Singh had turned the lives of his children, wife, and parents into a living nightmare.

The following day, Bhola Singh was summoned to court for his hearing. The courtroom was packed to the brim, with not even a sliver of space left to stand. Yet, the crowd swelled, eager to hear the judges' verdict and Bhola Singh's plea.

The courtroom buzzed with the hum of whispers and rustling papers as the judge, a stern figure of justice, entered and took his place at the bench. The gavel banged, commanding silence.

Judge: "Order in the court. We are gathered here to deliberate the case of Bhola Singh, accused of multiple heinous crimes, including poaching, abduction, and the exploitation of the impoverished and marginalized. Prosecution, you may proceed."

The prosecutor, a sharp and articulate woman named Advocate Thapa, rose to her feet. She adjusted her glasses, her eyes piercing through the dim light that filtered into the courtroom.

Advocate Thapa: "Your Honor, distinguished members of the jury, today we stand united in the pursuit of justice for those who cannot defend themselves. The evidence against the accused, Bhola Singh, is overwhelming and incontrovertible. We have testimonies, material evidence, and a history of criminal conduct that paints a vivid picture of his guilt."

She gestured towards a table laden with exhibits—photographs of the jungle, seized animal skins, stacks of money, and chains that once bound innocent children.

Advocate Thapa: "Bhola Singh has been a blight on this village, preying on the vulnerable and perpetuating a reign of terror. Let us not forget the seventeen children abducted under his orders, children whose lives are forever scarred by his insidious actions. We seek not only justice but a message that such malfeasance will not go unpunished."

The defence lawyer, Advocate Shreshtha, an older man with a grave demeanour, stood to respond.

Advocate Shreshtha: "Your Honor, my client, Bhola Singh, acknowledges that he has made mistakes. However, we must remember the fundamental principle of our legal system: every individual is innocent until proven guilty beyond a reasonable doubt. The prosecution's narrative is compelling, yet it relies heavily on circumstantial evidence. I implore this court to consider whether the evidence truly meets the burden of proof required for a conviction."

As the proceedings continued, witnesses were called to the stand. One by one, they recounted their harrowing experiences.

A frail woman, her face etched with sorrow, stepped up. She spoke in a voice trembling with emotion.

Witness 1: "Bhola Singh took my son. He was only twelve. We searched for him for days, but it was as if he had vanished into thin air. My boy was everything to me, and now my life is just a hollow shell."

Tears streamed down her face as she clutched a worn photograph of her child. The courtroom was silent, the weight of her words hanging in the air.

Next, a forest ranger took the stand. His voice was steady, filled with a righteous anger.

Forest Ranger: "I've seen the aftermath of Bhola Singh's poaching expeditions. The bodies of majestic creatures left to rot; their skins torn from their flesh for profit. Our forest, once a sanctuary, has become a graveyard because of him."

He presented maps and reports detailing the extent of the devastation, the impact on local wildlife, and the ecosystem.

Advocate Shreshtha cross-examined each witness with precision, seeking to find cracks in their testimonies. He challenged the validity of the evidence, questioned the reliability of memories tainted by trauma, and argued for Bhola Singh's right to a fair trial.

Advocate Shreshtha: "Your Honor, we must be cautious of letting our emotions cloud our judgment. While the suffering described here is real and undeniable, we must ensure that justice is served through facts and not sentiments. There are no direct witnesses to the abductions attributed to my client, and the link between him and the poaching is tenuous at best."

Bhola Singh himself was called to the stand. His demeanour was unrepentant, a man hardened by years of power and impunity.

Bhola Singh: "I am not the monster they paint me to be. Yes, I have enemies, and I have done things I am not proud of, but these accusations are exaggerated. I have been made a scapegoat for the failures of others."

His words were met with murmurs of disbelief from the audience, many of whom had suffered under his reign.

The judge retired to his chambers, deliberating for what seemed like an eternity. When he returned, the air was thick with anticipation.

Judge: "Will the defendant please rise. Bhola Singh, this court has weighed the evidence presented by both sides. The testimonies of the victims, the material evidence, and your own admissions have led us to a clear conclusion. You have indeed perpetrated crimes against humanity and nature, causing irreparable harm."

The judge's voice was solemn, yet resolute.

Judge: "This court finds you guilty on all charges. Your actions have not only violated the law but have also inflicted untold suffering on the innocent. It is the duty of this court to ensure that justice is served, not just for the victims but for the community and future generations. You are hereby sentenced to life imprisonment without the possibility of parole."

A collective sigh of relief echoed through the courtroom. Justice, at long last, had prevailed.

As the courtroom emptied, Advocate Thapa approached the families of the victims, offering words of comfort. Advocate Shreshtha, though defeated, maintained his composure, knowing he had done his duty to the best of his ability.

Outside the courthouse, the villagers gathered, their faces a mixture of sorrow and hope. The children who had been rescued from Bhola Singh's clutches were embraced by their families, their future now looking a little brighter.

In the end, the trial of Bhola Singh was not just about one man's guilt, but a reaffirmation of the village's resilience and the enduring power of justice. The scars left by his crimes would take time to heal, but the verdict marked the beginning of a new chapter—a chapter where the oppressed found their voice and the guilty were held accountable.

As the sun set over the village, casting a golden hue over the landscape, there was a sense of closure. The wheels of justice had turned, and the community, though battered, stood stronger and more united than ever before.

20

Passionate Love Blossoms

Mahesh had meticulously prepared a special gift for Inara Wali: a stunning sari embroidered with silk, a pair of exquisite gold earrings, and a delicate gold chain. He carefully wrapped these treasures in a beautiful gift wrapper, concealing them further with a shabby outer cover to ensure the contents remained a secret. For days, he kept the packet close, waiting for the perfect moment to present his gift to her. In those times and in that part of the world, occasions like birthdays and Valentine's Day were not commonly celebrated among lovers.

One afternoon, just before the school was due to close, the skies opened up, and a heavy rain began to fall. The downpour was relentless, and as the school emptied, Mahesh seized the opportunity. He retrieved the packet from his office and approached Inara Wali quietly. Standing close to her, he leaned in and whispered in her ear, his lips so near that it seemed they might touch her skin. He told her that he wanted to see her in the sari and swiftly departed before she could respond.

The rain poured on, creating a rhythmic symphony that seemed to isolate them from the rest of the world. Inara Wali remained in the corridor; her figure illuminated by the soft, diffused light. The slanting rain fell gently on her cheeks, lips, and forehead, soaking her almost completely. Her drenched clothes clung to her body, subtly revealing the contours of her form and the delicate curve of her chests, which appeared tantalizingly through the fabric.

Mahesh, watching from a nearby window, was captivated by her ethereal beauty. She seemed transformed into a nymph, a celestial being dancing to the rhythm of the rain and wind. The sight filled him with an intense, almost unbearable desire. He struggled to contain the yearning that surged within him as he observed her standing there, seemingly unaware of the spell she had cast upon him.

The rain continued its relentless descent, creating a cocoon of intimacy around Inara Wali. The droplets traced paths down her skin, mingling with the warmth of her body. She was lost in the moment, a vision of natural grace and allure. Mahesh's heart pounded in his chest, each beat echoing his longing. The scene was a painting come to life, an embodiment of the perfect, untouchable beauty that stirred the deepest emotions in him.

For a while, time seemed to stand still. The rain fell, Inara Wali stood, and Mahesh watched. The world outside ceased to exist, leaving only the two of them connected by the unseen thread of desire and anticipation. Then, as abruptly as it had begun, the rain started to taper off, the heavy drops turning into a gentle drizzle.

In that brief span of time, everything had changed. The rain had washed away the mundane, leaving behind a moment of pure, unadulterated beauty and longing. Mahesh knew that the memory of Inara Wali standing in the rain, her form subtly revealed through her wet clothes, would stay with him forever. It was a vision he would revisit in his dreams, a tribute to the power of a single, perfect moment.

In a picturesque village where the clinch of modernity was yet to reach, Inara Wali, adorned with eagerness, returned home cradling a mysterious packet. The gentle rhythm of life pulsed through the narrow lanes as she made her way to the Panchayat library, a sanctuary of knowledge amidst the rustic simplicity. Here, amidst the flickering glow of kerosene lanterns, she awaited the moment to unveil the contents of the enigmatic parcel.

With the dawn, a concerto of keenness resonated within her as she delicately untied the bindings of the parcel, revealing treasures bestowed upon her by Mahesh. A symphony of astonishment played in her heart as she beheld the sophisticated embroidery of the saree and the glimmering jewels cushioned within. Joy overflowed her heart, uncontainable, as she revelled in the depth of Mahesh's affection.

Yet, amidst the radiance of her joy, shadows of doubt danced in the corners of her mind. Were these gifts too extravagant? Should she have accepted them? Questions swirled like leaves caught in a whirlwind, yet beneath the surface, she recognized the tender sentiments merged into each thread of the fabric, each gleam of the jewels. They were not merely gifts but tokens of Mahesh's devotion, his care, his tenderness.

Undecided, she draped herself in the finery gifted by Mahesh, feeling its weight upon her like the breathed caress of a summer breeze. As she gazed upon her reflection, she beheld a vision of ethereal beauty, a goddess adorned in the offerings of love.

The following day, as she graced the school with her presence, words of admiration trailed in her wake, affirming the enchantment she exuded. The day unfolded like a delicate bloom unfurling its petals, each moment suffused with the glow of newfound allure.

And then, as the day waned and the shadows grew long, she sought refuge in the sanctuary of Mahesh's office, where time itself seemed to pause in reverence of their burgeoning connection. His gratitude washed over her like a gentle tide, and in the intimacy of the moment, she dared to inquire of her appearance, only to find Mahesh retreat behind a veil of bashfulness.

In a gesture both playful and tender, Mahesh extended his hand, bridging the divide between them with a touch that sent tremors of delight cascading through her being. With a mouthed endearment and a playful tweak of her nose, he bestowed upon her a memory that would linger as sweet as the fragrance of wildflowers in the spring breeze.

As the evening sun dipped below the horizon, casting the world in hues of amber and gold, they parted ways, each carrying within their hearts the indelible imprint of a love blooming like the first blossoms of spring—a love adorned in the exquisite tapestry of firsts.

In the soundless passages of the school, amidst the hustle and bustle of students and staff, a silent dance of longing and passion unfolded between two souls, Mahesh and his beloved. Each day dawned with an insatiable desire to catch a glimpse of her, to bask in the radiance of her presence. For Mahesh, the mornings lacked their usual lustre if he hadn't beheld her, if he hadn't felt the warmth of her gaze upon him. She became the focal point of his world, eclipsing all others in significance.

Her dedication to her duties was unparalleled. Assigned tasks were executed with meticulous care, her footsteps tracing a familiar path to his office, where their destinies intertwined amidst the papers and pens. Morning rituals saw her arrival, a sign of light to illuminate the day ahead, as she briefed him on the children under her mentorship. And in the moments that followed, as the school assembly commenced, she stood faithfully behind him, a silent scout of support.

But their interactions extended beyond the confines of duty. As visitors sought guidance and admissions, she sought his counsel, their encounters becoming a toil of shared moments. With familiarity came a blossoming bond, one that transcended the boundaries of professionalism. Laughter danced freely between them, words flowing like a gentle stream, carrying with them the weight of unspoken desires.

Their connection deepened with each passing day, expressed through stolen glances and fleeting touches. In the halcyon moments of solitude, they found solace in each other's cuddle, their lips meeting in a tender exchange of affection. Love, in its infinite wisdom, had completed its circle, uniting them together in a shared passion and devotion.

Mahesh's endearment, "baby," whispered softly in moments of intimacy, echoed her own term of endearment, "honey," a sweet creation of affection shared between them. Their love, once a fragile bud, had blossomed into a resplendent flower, its petals unfurling in the warmth of their devotion.

As they walked hand in hand through the corridors of the school, their love shone like a flare, illuminating the path ahead with its radiant glow. And in each other's arms, they found sanctuary, their hearts entwined in a bond that transcended time and space. For Mahesh and his beloved, theirs was a love story written in the stars, a demonstration to the power of love to conquer all.

On a serene Saturday, when the bustling corridors of academia lay quiet and the echoes of scholarly discourse were but a faint memory, a select few souls found themselves drawn to the sanctuary of the school library. Among them was Inara Wali, a diligent seeker of knowledge, her determination unwavering even on days of repose.

As she immersed herself in the pursuit of her scholarly duties, the library gradually became populated by others of kindred spirit: students with lingering assignments, teachers with papers to grade, all seeking to tame the relentless march of academic obligations.

In this hallowed space of learning, where the scent of ancient tomes mingled with the hushed whispers of scholarly endeavour, a scene of unexpected camaraderie unfolded. Mahesh, a figure of quiet contemplation, made his presence known as he settled into a solitary chair, his demeanour inviting discourse.

And so, amidst the weighty tomes and the flickering glow of reading lamps, a conversation blossomed—the threads of societal norms and the complexities of human relationships. The topic at hand, noble and contentious in equal measure, danced upon the lips of the gathered intellectuals: the interplay between caste, marriage, and the legal intricacies therein.

Inara Wali and Mahesh, each possessed of a keen intellect and a fervent passion for justice, found themselves embroiled in a spirited debate. With words as their weapons and reason as their shield, they delved deep into the heart of the matter, probing the nuances of tradition and the bounds of legality with unwavering resolve.

As the hours waned and the shadows grew long, the library echoed with the symphony of minds engaged in earnest discourse—an authentication to the enduring power of knowledge to illuminate, to challenge, and to inspire. And amidst the pages of history and the whispers of wisdom, the seeds of understanding were sown, nurturing the promise of a brighter, more inclusive tomorrow.

In the quietude of the school library, Mahesh and Inara Wali sat amidst shelves laden with books, the soft rustle of pages turning creating a soothing backdrop to their conversation. Mahesh sighed, gazing at the rows of knowledge, and began, "The world seems so vast and beautiful, yet within it, we humans create such divisions. What do you think, Inara Wali, about inter-caste marriages and their place in our society?" Inara Wali smiled warmly, her eyes reflecting wisdom as she responded, "Ah, Mahesh, a topic as old as civilization itself. Inter-caste marriage, a bond transcending man-made boundaries, has often been a subject of intense scrutiny. Historically, caste has been a rigid structure, deeply rooted in our socio-religious fabric. Yet, love and human connection have always sought to defy these constraints."

Mahesh nodded, his thoughts drifting to ancient tales. "Indeed. Our scriptures and history reflect both the rigidity and the rebellion against such norms. Take the story of Shakuntala and Dushyanta from the Mahabharata. Despite being from different backgrounds, their love transcended social barriers. Yet, our contemporary society seems to grapple with accepting such unions." Inara Wali thoughtfully replied, "True, Mahesh. The legal system today, however, offers a glimmer of hope. The Hindu Marriage Act of 1955 and the Special Marriage Act of 1954 in India recognize and protect inter-caste marriages. Legally, these marriages are valid and provide couples the right to marry regardless of caste distinctions. This is a progressive step towards a more inclusive society."

Mahesh acknowledged the point, "Yes, the law supports equality, but societal acceptance often lags behind. Families can be a major hurdle, rooted in centuries-old beliefs and customs. The fear of ostracism and the loss of social standing compel many to oppose such unions." Inara Wali, with a hint of determination in her voice, added, "You're right, Mahesh. It's a complex interplay of tradition, fear, and sometimes ignorance. Yet, the winds of change are blowing. Education and awareness are powerful tools.

"Baba Sahib Ambedkar's life indeed exemplifies the possibility of change," Mahesh mused. "He envisioned a society where caste would no longer dictate personal relationships or societal roles. But how do we accelerate this change, Inara Wali?" She responded with conviction, "It starts with us, Mahesh. By fostering dialogue, promoting empathy, and educating the younger generations, we can bridge the chasms of prejudice. Celebrating stories of inter-caste marriages can also inspire many. Literature, cinema, and art play significant roles in shaping public perception.

Mahesh smiled, "Art does have a unique power to touch hearts and change minds. Philosophically, it reminds me of the concept of 'Vasudhaiva Kutumbakam' – the world is one family. If we embrace this ideology, caste barriers would seem trivial." Inara Wali agreed, "Precisely. The idea of universal kinship and the interconnectedness of all human beings can dismantle the foundations of casteism. But it requires persistent effort and the courage to stand against deep-seated prejudices. Every inter-caste marriage that succeeds becomes an ideal of hope, slowly but surely changing societal norms."

Reflectively, Mahesh added, "Change is indeed a slow process, but it's heartening to see the progress. Legally, inter-caste marriages are protected, but the real victory will be when they are celebrated without a second thought, where love is the only binding force considered." Inara Wali smiled, her eyes twinkling with hope, "And that day will come, Mahesh. As long as there are individuals like us who believe in equality and work towards it, the dream of a caste-free society will become a reality. Let us continue to be the change we wish to see."

They sat in contemplative silence, surrounded by the wisdom of ages, the library standing as an endorsement to their resolve and the future they envisioned – where humanity thrives, unbound by caste, in the embrace of love and equality.

Their closeness and familiarity became the talk of the town. Whispers spread like wildfire, with villagers speculating whether their bond would blossom into love or marriage. Such developments, the gossipers argued, could tarnish the esteemed reputation of Mukhiya Jee and cause Inara Wali to lose her standing within the community. As a widow, she already faced societal scrutiny, and any misstep could force her to leave the village with her family. Traditional norms dictated that widows should live under strict constraints, and yet, Inara Wali seemed to defy these expectations with her demeanour and spirit.

Rumours soon turned malicious, suggesting that her confidence and grace stemmed from illicit relationships with multiple men. These whispers gained momentum, asserting that her walk, her looks, and her behaviour were all signs of her indiscretions. Mukhiya Jee, upon hearing these sordid tales, sought the truth from his sources. His inquiries confirmed that Inara Wali and Mahesh shared a deep affection for each other, with Mahesh's feelings particularly intense.

Mukhiya Jee took decisive action. Summoning Inara Wali, he informed her that only formally qualified individuals were permitted to work in the village school. As a result, her services were no longer required. However, he extended an offer for her to work as an office clerk in his Panchayat Office, a position that would keep her under closer watch and away from the school. He instructed her to hand over all responsibilities to Mahesh and to begin her new role the next day. Helpless against his authority, Inara Wali had no choice but to comply.

The separation of these two kindred spirits was swift and painful. Mukhiya Jee also directed Mahesh to hire more qualified men to support the school, rather than relying on women. The abruptness of these decisions cast a pall over their once joyful lives, plunging them into despair. Their meetings, once frequent and filled with warmth, became rare and brief, sometimes separated by weeks.

Despite the forced distance, the strength of their love endured. Though they had to learn to live apart, their bond grew only stronger, fortified by the trials they faced. Each brief encounter became a cherished moment, each stolen glance a reminder of the love that persisted against all odds.

Inara Wali's new role in the Panchayat Office was a stark contrast to her previous position at the school. The bureaucratic environment was stifling compared to the lively atmosphere she once enjoyed. She missed the laughter of the children, the sense of purpose that came with teaching. Now, her days were filled with monotonous clerical work, a constant reminder of the price she paid for loving Mahesh.

Mahesh, on the other hand, found it difficult to fill the void left by her absence. The school, once a place of collaboration and shared dreams, now felt empty and cold. The new hires, though qualified, lacked the passion and connection that Inara Wali brought to her work. His heart ached with each passing day, longing for the simple joy of her presence.

Their love story, though suspended, was far from over. Each obstacle they faced only fuelled their determination to remain connected. They adapted to their new circumstances, finding creative ways to communicate and support each other from afar. Secret letters, hidden messages, and fleeting encounters became the lifelines that kept their love alive.

The village continued to abuzz with speculation and gossip, but Inara Wali and Mahesh learned to tune it out. They found solace in their unwavering commitment to each other, drawing strength from their shared dreams and whispered promises. Their love, though tested by time and circumstance, remained a fire of prospect in a world that sought to keep them apart.

As the seasons changed, so did their resolve. They became adept at navigating the constraints placed upon them, finding moments of joy in the midst of their sorrow. Their love story, though paused by external forces, continued to flourish in the quiet spaces of their hearts. And in those rare moments when they were together, the world seemed to fall away, leaving only the two of them, bound by a love that was unbreakable.

In the end, it was their love that prevailed. Mukhiya Jee's attempts to separate them only strengthened their bond, proving that true love cannot be confined by societal norms or arbitrary rules. Inara Wali and Mahesh's story became evidence to the power of love and resilience, inspiring those around them to believe in the possibility of enduring happiness despite the challenges they faced.

21

Unseen Chains: Ideological Battle

Over the years, many students from the village and its surrounding areas, including Inara Wali, achieved academic success and graduated. The more affluent families sent their children to nearby towns such as Janakpur, Kathmandu, Lumbini, and Birganj in Nepal. Some even ventured further, crossing borders into Indian cities like Sitamarhi, Darbhanga, Patna, and Banaras. Those who couldn't afford to travel exerted themselves privately to complete their education. In this collective pursuit of knowledge, Shri Ram Avatar and Shri Govind Paswan remained steadfast pillars of support, offering invaluable guidance and assistance with examinations.

Nepal's journey towards educational advancement had been fraught with challenges. The country had endured long and difficult phases in its education system. For generations, the kings of Nepal were not truly sovereign, their authority reduced to mere ceremonial rubber stamps under the oppressive rule of the Rana dynasty. The Ranas, who wielded absolute power, systematically denied education to the common people. Education was a privilege reserved for the royals, high-ranking royal servants, and the affluent who managed to curry favour with the ruling elite. As a result, Nepal was left with a sparse educational infrastructure, boasting only a handful of schools and even fewer colleges. The country's sole university, Tribhuvan University, was meagrely equipped, struggling to meet the demands of a growing population hungry for knowledge.

Despite these formidable obstacles, the desire for education among Nepal's people remained undiminished. In the absence of state support, communities and individuals took it upon themselves to ensure that their children received the education they deserved. Affluent families, recognizing the limitations within Nepal, sought opportunities abroad, sending their children to study in India. This migration for education became a sign to their unwavering commitment to academic achievement and personal growth.

Those who stayed behind faced a different set of challenges. With limited resources and institutional support, they relied on personal initiative and community solidarity. Shri Ram Avatar and Shri Govind Paswan emerged as standards of optimism during these trying times. Their dedication to assisting students with their studies and examinations became a cornerstone of the community's educational endeavours. They provided not just academic support but also inspired a sense of perseverance and pliability among the students.

The impact of this grassroots movement towards education was profound. Students from various communities, including the marginalized Inara Wali, broke through barriers of caste and class to pursue their dreams. Their mutual efforts began to slowly transform the educational landscape of Nepal. Each graduate represented not just personal achievement but also a victory against the historical oppression that had long denied education to the masses.

As time passed, these educated individuals returned to their communities, bringing with them new ideas and knowledge. They became catalysts for change, advocating for better educational facilities and more inclusive policies. Their experiences in Nepal and abroad highlighted the stark contrasts in educational opportunities, fuelling their determination to bridge the gap and improve the system for future generations.

In essence, the story of education in Nepal is one of resilience and relentless pursuit of knowledge. It is a narrative shaped by historical struggles and personal triumphs, where community support played a crucial role in overcoming systemic challenges. The contributions of individuals like Shri Ram Avatar and Shri Govind Paswan underscore the importance of mentorship and guidance in this journey. Their unwavering commitment helped lay the foundation for a more educated and empowered Nepal, fostering a legacy that continues to inspire future generations.

The ascent of the Rana family in Nepal is a tale steeped in ambition, strategy, and an era of autocratic rule that indelibly shaped the country's history. This narrative unfurls amidst the 19th and 20th century Nepal, a period marked by both transformation and clamour.

The Rana dynasty's rise began with a singular, decisive event known as the Kot Massacre in 1846. Jung Bahadur

Kunwar, who later adopted the surname Rana, orchestrated this bloodbath in the royal courtyard (the Kot), leading to the extermination of numerous noblemen and rivals. This act of ruthless consolidation of power paved the way for Jung Bahadur to become the de facto ruler of Nepal. He assumed the title of Prime Minister and Commander-in-Chief, effectively reducing the monarch to a figurehead.

Jung Bahadur Rana's ascent was underpinned by his military acumen and political shrewdness. He capitalized on the existing discontent among the military factions and nobility, presenting himself as the stabilizing force amid the chaos that had plagued the Kathmandu Valley. His leadership was marked by the introduction of the Muluki Ain (The Law of the Land) in 1854, a comprehensive legal code that sought to systematize the administration and judiciary, echoing his vision of a centralized and autocratic state.

The Ranas ruled with a feudal and patriarchal ideology, drawing heavily from their martial heritage and the Hindu caste system. Their governance philosophy was rooted in absolute control, ensuring that power remained within the family through a hierarchical and hereditary structure. This concentration of power was symbolized by the creation of a parallel government within the Rana household, where senior family members held key positions.

Their autocratic rule was characterized by a blend of regressive and progressive policies. On one hand, the Ranas were staunch conservatives, resisting any form of democratization or political reform that could threaten their hegemony. On the other, they were pragmatists who recognized the importance of modernization, albeit in a controlled manner. Jung Bahadur's visit to Europe in 1850 influenced his approach to governance, leading to selective modernization initiatives such as the establishment of a Western-style military and the introduction of Western education for the elite.

The Rana regime spanned over a century, marked by the reigns of several influential prime ministers, each contributing to the dynasty's legacy:

Jung Bahadur Rana (1846-1877): The architect of Rana rule, whose decisive actions and diplomatic manoeuvres established the family's dominance. His policies aimed at strengthening central authority and suppressing dissent.

Ranodip Singh Kunwar (1877-1885): Jung Bahadur's younger brother, whose tenure was marked by internal family conflicts and external pressures, leading to his assassination and further consolidation of power by his successors.

Bir Shamsher Jang Bahadur Rana (1885-1901): Known for his administrative reforms and infrastructural projects, including the establishment of the first college in Nepal, he sought to modernize the state apparatus.

Chandra Shamsher Jang Bahadur Rana (1901-1929): His tenure was characterized by significant social reforms, including the abolition of slavery in 1924. He also pursued diplomatic relations, balancing between British India and the emerging global powers.

Juddha Shamsher Jang Bahadur Rana (1932-1945): A controversial figure, his rule saw the severe suppression of political dissent and the devastating 1934 Nepal–Bihar earthquake, which prompted significant reconstruction efforts.

The Rana regime's decline was precipitated by both internal and external factors. Internally, the rigid autocracy and resistance to political reform bred widespread discontent among the populace and the rising educated middle class. The suppression of political movements and civil liberties fuelled resentment and opposition.

Externally, the geopolitical landscape was shifting. The rise of Indian nationalism and the subsequent independence movement provided both inspiration and practical support to Nepalese revolutionaries. The establishment of the Nepali Congress in 1947, a political party dedicated to the establishment of democracy, marked a significant turn in Nepal's political evolution. The Ranas' inability to adapt to these changes accentuated their growing isolation.

The tipping point came with the revolution of 1950-51. The assassination of King Tribhuvan's close ally by Rana operatives sparked a rebellion, leading the king to seek asylum in India. This moves galvanized anti-Rana forces, culminating in widespread uprisings supported by the Nepali Congress and exiled leaders. The Indian government's mediation and the subsequent Delhi Accord of 1951 led to the return of King Tribhuvan and the establishment of a coalition government, marking the official end of Rana rule.

The post-Rana period ushered in a nascent democracy, with King Tribhuvan reinstating the Shah monarchy's constitutional role. The transition, however, was fraught with challenges. The new government grappled with balancing modern democratic aspirations with the entrenched feudalistic structures left behind by the Ranas.

The Rana period in Nepal is a complex chapter in the nation's history, characterized by both significant achievements and profound failures. The Ranas' legacy is dual-edged. Their contributions to modernization—such as infrastructure development, legal codification, and educational reforms—cannot be overlooked. The establishment of Nepal's first postal service, construction of roads, and the introduction of modern administrative practices are endorsements to their efforts at progress.

Conversely, their autocratic rule stifled political freedoms and perpetuated social inequalities. The feudal and caste-based hierarchies they reinforced left deep societal scars. The suppression of dissent and the concentration of power within a narrow elite led to widespread disenfranchisement and delayed the democratic maturation of Nepal.

The Rana period also saw significant figures whose actions and policies continue to evoke mixed reactions. Jung Bahadur Rana's legacy, for instance, is one of both admiration for his statecraft and criticism for his ruthless consolidation of power. Chandra Shamsher's abolition of slavery is lauded, yet his repressive measures against political opponents are condemned. These contradictions are reflective of the broader complexities within Rana rule.

At the heart of Rana governance was a deep-seated belief in the necessity of strong, centralized control to maintain order and stability. This philosophy was influenced by a mix of traditional Hindu statecraft, which emphasized hierarchical governance, and realpolitik, which prioritized pragmatic and often hardnosed measures to preserve power. The Ranas saw themselves as custodians of Nepalese sovereignty, maintaining a delicate balance between appeasing British India and asserting their authority domestically.

Their governance model was inherently patriarchal and elitist, with a clear demarcation between the ruling elite and the general populace. This was reflected in their policies, which often prioritized the interests of the elite while marginalizing the masses. Education and modernization efforts were typically confined to the Rana family and their close associates, ensuring that the broader population remained subservient and less likely to challenge their rule.

The Rana family's rise and fall are emblematic of the broader dynamics of power, resistance, and change in Nepalese history. Their century-long rule left an indelible mark on the nation's political, social, and cultural fabric. While their contributions to modernization were significant, their autocratic and feudalistic governance ultimately sowed the seeds of their downfall.

The legacy of the Ranas is a poignant reminder of the complexities inherent in autocratic rule and the enduring struggle for democratic governance. It highlights the importance of inclusive and equitable political systems, where power is not concentrated within a narrow elite but shared among the broader populace.

In reflecting on the Rana era, one is reminded of the delicate balance between tradition and modernity, authority and liberty, stability and progress. The Ranas' story is not just a historical account but a timeless lesson in the perennial quest for justice, freedom, and the right to self-determination. As Nepal continues to steer its path in the modern world, the echoes of its Rana past serve as both a cautionary tale and a source of reflection on the values and principles that should guide its future.

In the aftermath of His Majesty's government, the landscape of the nation bore the indelible scars and intricate mesh of ideologies they left behind. These entrenched beliefs had, over time, forged an invisible chain that shackled the collective consciousness of the people. It took decades of relentless effort to dismantle these barriers, to break free from the constraints that had long stifled progress and unity.

The nation's journey toward cohesion was fraught with numerous challenges. Economically, they were bound by the limitations of a system that had been designed to serve colonial interests rather than foster indigenous growth. The land itself, marked by arbitrary borders and contested territories, bore witness to the geographical strife that fragmented communities and hindered development. Politically, the nascent state grappled with the remnants of autocratic rule, striving to establish a governance system that was truly representative of its diverse populace.

Yet, perhaps the most formidable obstacle was the ideological constraint that permeated every aspect of life. The colonial legacy had ingrained a sense of inferiority and division among the people, perpetuating a social hierarchy that was antithetical to the principles of equality and justice. Overcoming this ideological divide required a profound transformation, a reawakening of the collective spirit that emphasized common humanity and shared destiny.

To bring the citizens under one unified banner, where each individual could claim an equal share of opportunities, was a monumental task. It was imperative that no one be denied justice, that every voice be heard and every grievance addressed. The vision was clear: a nation where all had enough to eat and wear, where the basic needs of life were met, thus liberating minds to think freely and dream expansively under the canopy of a free sky.

In this new dawn, the foundation of a just society was laid. The effort to ensure that every citizen had adequate sustenance and clothing was not merely a matter of survival but a prerequisite for freedom of thought and innovation. With these fundamental needs secured, people could aspire to higher ideals, contribute meaningfully to the nation's growth, and partake in the shared journey toward prosperity.

This era marked the emergence of a nation where the collective endeavour of its people began to bear fruit. The infrastructure, both ideological and physical, slowly took shape. Roads and bridges connected previously isolated regions, facilitating trade and cultural exchange. Educational institutions sprang up, nurturing a new generation of thinkers, leaders, and innovators. Healthcare systems were established, ensuring that the wellbeing of every citizen was safeguarded.

The sense of unity that began to permeate the national consciousness was a testament to the resilience and determination of the people. Communities that had once been divided by artificial barriers now worked together to build a common future. The ideals of equality and justice were not just enshrined in laws but were becoming a lived reality, as people from all walks of life began to see themselves as integral parts of a greater whole.

In this vibrant new nation, the contributions of every individual were recognized and valued. The scars of the past, while not forgotten, served as reminders of the journey undertaken and the progress achieved. The once fragmented society was now bound by a shared commitment to the principles of liberty, equality, and fraternity.

As the nation continued to evolve, it became a model of what could be achieved when a people, united by common purpose and mutual respect, work together towards a brighter future. This transformation was not just a triumph of governance but a verification to the resolute spirit of the human heart. The nation stood as a symbol of resilience, evidence to the power of unity, and a shining example of the prosperity that could be achieved when every citizen had the opportunity to contribute to the common good.

Change in society is seldom the product of mere aspirations, policy declarations, or grandiloquent speeches. True transformation demands an unyielding effort to shift the collective mindset. Despite numerous obstacles, there was progress, albeit at a sluggish pace. The quest for dignified survival and equal opportunities was fought in every district, village, and neighbourhood. Inara Wali – now a graduate with a wealth of experience working for her community – stood composed and organized alongside her equally educated friends, ready to shoulder the grander tasks that lay ahead. Their education had not only empowered them to better understand the intricacies of law and society but had also instilled in them refined habits, sophistication in speech, and elegance in conduct. It became increasingly challenging to distinguish them from the affluent.

The spirit of life in the village had taken a transformative turn. The children of the wealthy, both growing and young, displayed a newfound amity and a sense of equality and togetherness. Although their elders did not always endorse this escalating acceptance, they had little choice but to adapt to the evolving culture of the village. Education had brought with it joy, aspirations, and a deep-seated bond of understanding.

Puttali Gacch, a tree that seemed to have been blessed by heavenly forces, stood as a hushed picket to these changes. It offered its shade to all who sought its refuge, fully aware of the chronology of events that had unfolded under its spurs. It was the guiding light for many, especially for Inara Wali.

The village, with its serene landscape and the ancient Puttali Gacch at its heart, was undergoing a metamorphosis. The grand tree, with its sprawling branches and thick foliage, had seen generations come and go, each leaving behind a unique imprint on its enduring bark. The villagers often gathered under its vast canopy, finding solace and shade, sharing stories and dreams, seeking advice and wisdom.

Inara Wali and her companions found in the Puttali Gacch a symbol of their struggle and their hardiness. It was under this tree that they often met, strategizing about how to tackle the various challenges their community faced. The tree, with its deep roots and towering presence, mirrored their own resolve and aspirations. It stood enduring spirit and unremitting pursuit of equality and justice.

Their journey was not without its trials. The entrenched norms and prejudices of the older generation often clashed with the progressive ideas of the younger ones. Yet, there was an undeniable shift in the air. The younger generation, with their education and enlightened views, were breaking down barriers, fostering a sense of unity and mutual respect that had been long absent.

Education had been the catalyst for this transformation. It had opened doors to new possibilities, broadened horizons, and instilled a sense of confidence and self-worth. Inara Wali and her friends embodied this change. They spoke with clarity and conviction, their words carrying the weight of their experiences and the promise of a brighter future. They conducted themselves with a grace and dignity that commanded respect and admiration.

The elders, while hesitant and often resistant, could not ignore the winds of change sweeping through the village. The harmonious relationships between their children and those from less affluent backgrounds were a new social order taking root. Slowly but surely, they began to adapt, realizing that the future of the village lay in containing these changes.

Puttali Gacch continued to be an inspiration. It stood tall, its leaves rustling in the wind to those who sought its shelter. It had witnessed the struggles and triumphs of the villagers, absorbing their stories into its very being. For Inara Wali, the tree was a source of strength and a reminder of the progress they had made.

The village was not just a collection of houses and fields; it was a living, breathing entity, evolving with each passing day. The changes, though gradual, were profound. The bonds of friendship and understanding that had formed were reshaping the social fabric, creating a more comprehensive and equitable community.

There was a sense of hope and anticipation in the air. The journey was far from over, but with leaders like Inara Wali at the helm, the future seemed promising.

The spirit of the village, nurtured by education and a shared vision of equality, was blossoming, much like the venerable tree that stood watch over them all.

22

Prison Power Dynamics

Bhola Singh had been in prison for a considerable time now, much to the delight of the villagers who relished his absence. His wife, burdened by the disgrace he had brought upon their family, had abandoned their village home, seeking refuge with her parents. The house remained locked, a silent tribute to their fallen honour. Over time, the villagers had nearly erased him from their collective memory, finding solace in the tranquillity his absence afforded.

Inside the prison walls, however, a different narrative unfolded. Bhola Singh presented himself as a reformed man, one whose demeanour exuded gentleness and compliance, aimed at winning the Favor of the authorities. Yet, beneath this facade, he was orchestrating a sinister scheme. He meticulously brainwashed a substantial number of fellow inmates, crafting a formidable alliance within the prison. Senior officers, rarely present, remained oblivious to his machinations. The ordinary guards, enticed by bribes or other incentives, sang his praises, ensuring his nefarious activities went unnoticed.

The prison housed a motley crew of criminals – robbers, thieves, impostors, murderers – each bearing unique skills and dark pasts. The administration, in a bid to instil some semblance of order, engaged prisoners in vocational training, assigning them roles as labourers, librarians, carpenters, and tailors, accompanied by a modest wage. But within this structured chaos, Bhola Singh thrived on manipulation and domination. He commandeered his peers' rations and comforts, coercing them into servitude. Massages, laundry services, and the appropriation of their meagre comforts and allowances were all extracted under his tyrannical rule.

A master of division, Bhola Singh stratified the inmates along socio-economic and communal lines. He decreed that only the affluent among them could enter the kitchen, relegating cooking duties exclusively to them. Meals were served in a strictly hierarchical order – first to the affluent, and only afterwards to the others, who ate in a subsequent shift. The laborious tasks of washing kitchenware and maintaining cleanliness were imposed upon prisoners from less privileged communities. These arrangements, executed with cunning precision, unfolded right under the noses of the jail authorities, who remained blissfully ignorant of the brewing inequities.

Bhola Singh's dominion within the prison was a stark contrast to the external facade of a reformed individual. His actions behind bars revealed a calculated strategist, one who thrived on exploiting the weaknesses and hierarchies within the prison system. The guards, swayed by his deceptive charm and monetary incentives, turned a blind eye to the injustices unfolding in their midst.

The prison, a microcosm of society's darker elements, became Bhola Singh's kingdom. He wielded power with an iron fist, his authority unchallenged by those too weak or too fearful to oppose him. Each day, the prison bore silent witness to the subjugation and division orchestrated by Bhola Singh, a man who's cunning and ruthlessness knew no bounds.

Despite the regimented activities and supposed reformative efforts within the prison, Bhola Singh's influence corrupted the intended order. His ability to manipulate and control his environment showcased a disturbing resilience and adaptability. The hierarchy he imposed not only exacerbated existing divisions but also created a palpable tension among the inmates.

Yet, the outside world remained unaware of the true nature of Bhola Singh's imprisonment. To the villagers and his estranged wife, he was a disgraced figure, an unfortunate chapter in their past. Inside the prison, however, he continued to wield a power that belied his supposed reformation, a power that fed on fear, manipulation, and the darker aspects of human nature.

The narrative of Bhola Singh's life in prison was full of complexities of human behaviour and the dichotomy between appearance and reality. His story, unfolding within the grim confines of a prison, is a chilling reminder of how power and control can corrupt, turning even a place of supposed rehabilitation into a bastion of inequality and exploitation.

The sun filtered through the narrow, barred windows of the superintendent's office, casting a fractured light onto the stark, utilitarian furnishings. The room was a study in bureaucratic austerity, its walls adorned with certificates and plaques that extolled years of diligent service. Behind a large, imposing desk sat Shri Mohan Lal, Jail Superintendent, a man of stern countenance but perceptive eyes, who had summoned Bhola Singh for a conversation.

Bhola Singh entered the room with measured steps, his demeanour the very picture of humility and respect. He was dressed in the plain uniform of the prison, but his posture exuded an air of quiet confidence. The superintendent gestured to a chair opposite his desk, inviting Bhola to sit.

"Bhola Singh," began the superintendent, his voice a rich baritone that filled the room. "I have heard many commendations about your behaviour and the positive influence you seem to exert on your fellow inmates. I wanted to hear from you directly about the state of affairs in the jail."

Bhola Singh inclined his head slightly, a modest smile playing on his lips. "Thank you, sir. I strive to make amends for my past mistakes by helping to maintain peace and order here. The inmates, for the most part, are cooperative and eager to learn new skills. We have established a sense of community and mutual respect."

The superintendent nodded, leaning back in his chair. "That is commendable, Bhola. I understand you have been instrumental in organizing various activities and ensuring the smooth functioning of daily routines. Can you elaborate on these initiatives?"

"Certainly, sir," Bhola replied, his voice steady and sincere. "We have set up a system where prisoners can engage in vocational training that suits their skills and interests. For example, we have carpenters, tailors, and librarians among us. These roles not only keep the inmates occupied but also prepare them for a productive life once they are released. We also have a rotation system for kitchen duties, ensuring that everyone contributes to the community."

The superintendent's eyes narrowed slightly, though his expression remained neutral. "I've also heard some concerns, Bhola. There are whispers of divisions among the inmates based on economic status and community lines. How do you address such issues?"

Bhola's smile didn't waver, though a fleeting shadow crossed his eyes. "Such divisions are inevitable in any society, sir, but we have taken steps to minimize their impact. We encourage inclusivity and fairness. Meals, for instance, are served in shifts to manage the large number of inmates efficiently. It is not about division, but about practical management."

The superintendent's gaze bore into Bhola, searching for any cracks in the facade. "And what about the allegations of favouritism and coercion? There are reports suggesting that certain inmates receive preferential treatment and that some are forced into labour."

"Such allegations are unfortunate misunderstandings," Bhola said smoothly. "In any system, there will be those who feel slighted or aggrieved. We do our best to ensure fair treatment for all. The so-called favouritism is merely a reflection of the natural order where those who exhibit leadership and cooperation often find themselves in positions of greater responsibility. As for coercion, sir, I assure you that any labour performed here is voluntary and compensated fairly."

The superintendent's lips pressed into a thin line, considering Bhola's words carefully. "I appreciate your Candor, Bhola Singh. However, it is my duty to ensure that the principles of justice and equality are upheld within these walls. I will be conducting a thorough review of these concerns to ensure that no inmate is being unfairly treated or coerced."

"Of course, sir," Bhola Singh responded, his tone unchangingly respectful. "I welcome any investigation that can help improve the conditions here. My only aim is to contribute positively to the environment and help my fellow inmates find a path to redemption."

The superintendent nodded, though the suspicion in his eyes had not entirely dissipated. "Very well, Bhola. I will take your words into consideration. You may return to your duties."

Bhola Singh stood, offering a respectful nod before exiting the office. As he walked down the dim corridor back to the main part of the prison, his mind churned with thoughts. The conversation had gone as well as he had hoped, but he knew that maintaining his carefully constructed image would require continued vigilance and cunning.

The superintendent watched him leave; his mind equally occupied. He had seen men like Bhola Singh before, men who could wear the mask of reform while hiding a core of manipulation and deceit. He resolved to delve deeper into the reality of Bhola's influence within the prison, determined to uncover the truth that lay beneath the surface.

Thus, the dance of deception and scrutiny continued, each man aware of the other's game, each preparing for the next move in a battle of wits and wills within the confining walls of the prison.

23

Elder's Retaliation and Consequences

Many young men and women received their education, eagerly absorbing knowledge with dreams of a brighter future. Despite their aspirations, the village and its neighbouring areas could not offer the employment opportunities they sought. Thus, these educated youths embarked on journeys to larger towns like Kathmandu, Janakpur, Pokhara, and Lumbini. Their ambitions carried some even further, to Indian cities such as Sitamarhi, Darbhanga, Muzaffarpur, Patna, and Delhi in pursuit of jobs.

The allure of stable employment led others to vie for government positions within Nepal. It was heartening to witness many of them securing roles in esteemed institutions such as Nepal Bank Limited, the National Bank of Nepal, and various departments of agriculture and education. Locally, some pursued careers in teaching, enriching the minds of the next generation, while others thrived in the health sector. Their success was a potential within the village, a hope for those who remained.

Moreover, a number of these young villagers qualified for industrial training and diploma courses in engineering, agriculture, and health—programs meticulously designed and sponsored by His Majesty's Government of Nepal. These job-oriented courses equipped them with specialized skills, further enhancing their employability. As a result, the migration of educated youth from the village became a common narrative, with only a handful staying behind to take up whatever employment was available locally.

The economic landscape of the village underwent a notable transformation. The financial conditions of the affluent and various other communities improved significantly. With newfound prosperity, families could afford better food, clothing, and other necessities, raising their standard of living.

When these young professionals returned to their village, often they were not alone. They came back married, their spouses accompanying them to seek the blessings of their elders. Such reunions were celebrated across all communities within the village. The parents and elders, though initially surprised, had little choice but to embrace these new family members. The wives were frequently educated, hailing from diverse backgrounds in terms of faith, origin, and social status, which added a rich cultural variety to the village.

The integration of these educated women into the village life brought about subtle yet significant changes. Their different perspectives and experiences began to influence local customs and practices. These women, having seen more of the world, often had progressive ideas that slowly started to take root in the village's social framework. The elders, though initially resistant to change, began to appreciate the fresh viewpoints these women introduced.

As the village adapted to these transformations, it also retained its deep-rooted traditions, creating a unique blend of old and new. Festivals were celebrated with renewed vigour, combining traditional rituals with new customs brought in by the new members of the community. This blending of cultures enriched the village, making it a microcosm of a broader, more diverse world.

The children of these new unions represented a fusion of cultures and ideas, embodying the future of the village. They grew up with the traditional wisdom of their grandparents and the modern perspectives of their parents. This duality prepared them to navigate both the local and wider worlds, poised to carry forward the legacy of their village while being equipped to face global challenges.

In the end, the village, though small and remote, became a symbol of adaptability. Its story was one of growth and transformation, driven by the aspirations of its young men and women. The journeys they undertook, the challenges they faced, and the successes they achieved were not just personal victories but a collective triumph for the entire community. This narrative of migration and return, acceptance and integration, painted a picture of a village in constant evolution, forever striving towards a better future while holding onto the essence of its past.

Though outwardly it seemed a narrative of triumph and progress, beneath the surface, the elders of such children harboured deep-seated resentment and responded in various ways. In the realm of newlywed women, particularly those whose faith, origin, or social standing did not align with the established norms, they faced severe ostracization. They were forbidden from participating in household worship rituals, relegated to the margins of family spirituality. Their eating and drinking utensils were segregated, a tangible symbol of their unwelcome presence. Men dined before women, adhering to a strict patriarchal hierarchy, and these newlywed brides were served separately, their isolation accentuated by the necessity to clean and store their utensils apart from the rest.

These unspoken but profoundly felt injustices rendered the lives of these women unbearably oppressive. They felt the sting of exclusion and the weight of discrimination in every aspect of their domestic existence. The dream of being with their husbands, of forging a new life together, often clashed with the harsh realities imposed by their in-laws. For many, it was a matter of bloodline and honour, the sacrosanct lineage that could not be tainted by an outsider's presence.

In the shadowy corners of these households, darker events unfolded. Elders, often in collusion with other family members, sometimes resorted to the ultimate violence—honour killings. These heinous acts were meticulously disguised as suicides, cloaked in silence and deceit. The community, already grappling with change, found itself mired in a new set of social problems. Families whose sons or daughters married outside their lineage were ostracized, creating a ripple effect of exclusion and intolerance. Though outwardly it seemed a narrative of triumph and progress, beneath the surface, the elders of such children harboured deep-seated resentment and responded in various ways. In the realm of newlywed women, particularly those whose faith, origin, or social standing did not align with the established norms, they faced severe ostracization. They were forbidden from participating in household worship rituals, relegated to the margins of family spirituality. Their eating and drinking utensils were segregated, a tangible symbol of their unwelcome presence. Men dined before women, adhering to a strict patriarchal hierarchy, and these newlywed brides were served separately, their isolation accentuated by the necessity to clean and store their utensils apart from the rest.

The societal landscape was undergoing a significant transformation. There was a palpable shift as families whose children pursued education or employment far from home were sternly warned against forming marital bonds outside their lineage. To enforce this, parents and other relatives made frequent visits to keep a vigilant eye, ensuring that the sanctity of their lineage remained uncompromised.

The harsh treatment of newlywed women, rooted in an obsession with purity and tradition, reflected a broader societal resistance to change. The elders, fiercely protective of their customs, viewed any deviation as a threat to their way of life. This rigid adherence to tradition created an environment where any breach, particularly in matters of marriage, was met with severe repercussions.

The narrative of success that initially appeared promising now revealed itself to be fraught with hidden tensions and unspoken grievances. Newlywed women, the supposed beneficiaries of this progress, found themselves at the centre of a storm of discontent. Their daily lives were marred by an intricate web of discrimination, isolation, and silent suffering.

This struggle against the constraints of tradition and the harsh judgment of the community painted a complex picture of rural life. It highlighted the immense pressure on families to conform to societal expectations and the lengths to which they would go to maintain their perceived honour and integrity. The stakes were high, and the consequences of defying these norms could be deadly.

The community's harsh stance on inter-lineage marriages extended beyond the confines of individual families. It was a collective effort to preserve a way of life that was increasingly under threat. This resistance to change, however, came at a significant cost, particularly for the women who bore the brunt of these rigid traditions.

As families navigated this tumultuous landscape, they were constantly reminded of the precarious balance between progress and tradition. The pressure to maintain the status quo was immense, and any deviation was met with swift and severe punishment. The story of these newlywed women, therefore, was not just a personal struggle but a reflection of the broader societal conflict between change and tradition.

In the end, the narrative of success that seemed so promising was overshadowed by the harsh realities of discrimination and violence. The newlywed women, who hoped for a better future, found themselves caught in a web of tradition and intolerance, their lives marked by silent suffering and unspoken despair. This story serves as a poignant reminder of the complexities and challenges of navigating the intersection of progress and tradition in rural communities.

The sun hung high in the cerulean sky, casting warm, golden rays over the verdant landscape. Women clad in vibrant saris moved gracefully, their laughter and chatter filling the air as they gathered around the village well. This well, a vital lifeline, served not only as a source of water but also as a social nexus where the womenfolk convened daily, exchanging news, gossip, and the occasional rumour.

Among them were Nandini and Suman, both newlywed brides steering the labyrinthine world of their in-laws' homes. Their paths had crossed many times at this well, but today they lingered, eager for a more extended conversation. The intimacy of shared burdens and the solace of mutual understanding drew them together.

Nandini, her eyes reflecting the weight of unspoken troubles, initiated the dialogue. "Suman, do you ever feel like an outsider in your own home? It's as if no matter how hard I try, I remain on the fringes."

Suman sighed, her shoulders drooping slightly under the weight of her own experiences. "Oh, Nandini, I know exactly how you feel. My in-laws make it clear that I don't belong. They've even separated my utensils. I eat alone, after everyone else. The isolation is unbearable."

The well, typically a site of vibrant, carefree chatter, seemed to hush in sympathy with their sombre conversation. Nandini nodded, her expression a mirror of Suman's despondency. "It's the same for me. I'm not allowed to worship at the family altar. They say it's because I'm not from their faith, but I think they just want to remind me of my place."

Their conversation, while steeped in melancholy, offered them a semblance of relief. Speaking their truths aloud, sharing their burdens, lessened the weight of their isolation. Suman's voice trembled slightly as she continued, "They watch me constantly, like a hawk. They fear I'll dishonour the family by mingling too much with those outside our lineage."

Nandini's eyes widened with a mixture of empathy and fear. "My family's the same. They've warned me about stepping out of line. And it's not just words. Have you heard the rumours about honour killings? There's talk that some deaths were not what they seemed."

Suman shivered, the gravity of Nandini's words sinking in. "I've heard whispers, but I thought—no, I hoped they were just rumours. To think that our lives could be in such danger, simply for being who we are..."

A silence settled between them, heavy and laden with the unsaid. The other women at the well, though engaged in their own conversations, seemed to sense the gravity of Nandini and Suman's exchange. A few glanced over, their expressions a mixture of curiosity and concern.

Breaking the silence, Suman tried to offer a semblance of hope. "I keep telling myself that things will change, that our generation will not hold on to such rigid traditions. But it's hard to see the light when you're constantly shrouded in darkness."

Nandini's eyes softened with a spark of determination. "Maybe we can be that change, Suman. Even in small ways. By supporting each other, by refusing to let these traditions break our spirits."

Suman managed a small smile, a glimmer of hope flickering in her eyes. "You're right, Nandini. We must be strong, for ourselves and for those who will come after us. This well, this place where we meet and talk, it's a start. We can share our stories, build our strength together."

The bond forming between Nandini and Suman was palpable, a thread of solidarity in the fabric of their constrained lives. Their dialogue continued, weaving between personal anecdotes and shared grievances, punctuated by moments of silent understanding.

As the sun began its descent, the women gathered their water pots, ready to return to their respective homes. But the weight of their conversation lingered, a silent struggle they endured and the resilient spirits that refused to be subdued.

Nandini and Suman parted ways, but their hearts were lighter, buoyed by the newfound connection. They had found in each other a kindred spirit, a reminder that even in the most oppressive circumstances, they were not alone. Their dialogue at the well-marked the beginning of a subtle but significant shift, a small rebellion against the rigid traditions that sought to confine them.

In the days that followed, their conversations continued, each meeting a reaffirmation of their resilience and a quiet defiance of the roles imposed upon them. They spoke not only of their struggles but also of their dreams, their hopes for a future where their daughters might drink from the same well without the taint of segregation.

The village well, once merely a source of water, had become a symbol of solidarity and strength, a place where two women found the courage to challenge the confines of their world. And in their shared words, they began to pile a new narrative, one of strength, hope, and quiet revolution.

24

First Civil Service Success

In a land where tradition often eclipsed progress, the news that both Mahesh and Inara Wali had qualified for the Nepal Civil Service Examination struck like a bolt of lightning. Mahesh, with his exceptional performance, had secured a commendable rank. Yet, it was Inara Wali who captured the public's imagination, despite her slightly lower position on the merit list. Her achievement was heralded not merely as personal triumph but as a historic milestone for her community.

As word spread, the media was ablaze with stories of Inara Wali's success. Newspapers dedicated columns to her journey, and radio broadcasts sang her praises. She was celebrated as the first individual from her community to conquer this prestigious examination, a feat that seemed to redefine the boundaries of possibility.

The village where Inara Wali had grown up buzzed with an unusual excitement. The news had barely settled when Mukhiya Jee, the village head, along with the schoolteachers, organized a grand ceremony. They adorned both Mahesh and Inara Wali with garlands, showering them with blessings and well-wishes for the path that lay ahead. It was a day of pride, not just for the families of the achievers but for the entire village.

For Inara Wali, this triumph was bittersweet. Her ascent meant leaving her village, a place that had shaped her and where she had, in turn, become a symbol of hope. As she prepared to depart for the training program, a cloud of apprehension impended over her community. The villagers, while elated at her success, harboured a deep-seated fear. They had enjoyed a newfound sense of freedom and equality, largely because of her influence and efforts. With her gone, they worried that the affluents might revert to their old oppressive ways, snatching away the liberties they had only just begun to enjoy.

Despite these fears, there was an undeniable sense of pride and anticipation. Inara Wali's absence was a gap that resonated deeply, but it also carried the promise of a brighter future. She was set to become the first female Chief District Officer of the district, a position that not only symbolized her personal achievement but also the breaking of new ground for women and marginalized communities.

Inara Wali's new role would empower her in ways previously unimagined. No longer would she need the endorsement of any Mukhiya Jee to enforce law and order or to implement government policies. Her authority would now span across the district, allowing her to champion causes and initiate reforms that could uplift the society as a whole, affluent and underprivileged alike.

As she embarked on her training, Inara Wali carried with her the hopes and fears of her community. The training programme was rigorous, designed to mould candidates into capable leaders. She faced it with the same determination that had seen her through the civil service examination. Each session, each lesson, was another step towards fulfilling the promise she had made to herself and her people.

The training period, though brief, was transformative. It honed her skills, broadened her perspective, and prepared her for the immense responsibility that awaited. She emerged more confident, her vision for her district clearer than ever. Inara Wali was ready to return, not just as a symbol of what could be achieved, but as a catalyst for real, tangible change.

Her return to the district as the Chief District Officer was nothing short of momentous. The anticipation was palpable. The very air seemed charged with a mix of hope and anxiety. As she stepped into her new role, the weight of her community's expectations rested heavily on her shoulders. Yet, Inara Wali stood undeterred. She understood that her position was not just an office but a platform to drive progress, to ensure that the freedoms her people had tasted would not be fleeting.

In her new capacity, Inara Wali began by establishing an open dialogue with the community. She made it clear that her door was always open, that their voices would be heard. Her approach was inclusive, recognizing that true progress could only be achieved through collective effort. She initiated programmes aimed at education, health, and economic development, focusing on the most vulnerable sections of society.

Her policies were met with resistance from the affluent quarters, as expected. But Inara Wali was prepared. With the law on her side and a resolute commitment to justice, she navigated the complexities of her role with finesse. She ensured that every decision, every policy, was a step towards a more equitable society.

As the months rolled on, the changes she implemented began to bear fruit. Schools saw higher attendance, healthcare services improved, and small businesses started to flourish. The community, once plagued by fear and uncertainty, began to thrive under her leadership. The respect she commanded was not just out of the authority of her office but out of the genuine impact she was making.

Inara Wali's journey was a demonstration to the power of perseverance and the importance of representation. She had broken barriers, not just for herself but for every girl in her village who now dreamed of a brighter future. Her success story was a flare, illuminating the path for others to follow.

Mahesh, too, continued to excel in his career, his achievements paralleling those of Inara Wali. Together, their stories inspired a generation, proving that with determination and hard work, the shackles of tradition could be broken.

In the end, Inara Wali's legacy was not just in the policies she implemented or the office she held. It was in the lives she touched, the dreams she nurtured, and the hope she instilled in her community. She had not only become a successful lady but a symbol of empowerment and change, a true harbinger of a new dawn for her people.

In the sun-dappled office of the Chief District Officer, two journalists, Prakash Kumar Ghimire from The Rising Sun and Pramila Shrestha from Gorkha Patra, were greeted with the warm smile of Ms. Sujata, a figure whose journey had captured the imagination of many. Prakash began the interview, expressing their gratitude for the opportunity to speak with her. Ms. Sujata, reflecting her characteristic grace, thanked them and welcomed the chance to share her story.

Pramila initiated the conversation by inquiring about Ms. Sujata's early life and the motivations that steered her towards the civil services. With a contemplative look, Sujata delved into her past, painting a vivid picture of her small village, where opportunities were limited, and traditions often stifled progress. Despite these challenges, she was blessed with poor parents who valued her and stored a thousand dreams for her. She spoke with reverence about key figures like Mukhiya Jee, Shri Ram Avatar, and Shri Govind Paswan. Mukhiya Jee, the visionary community leader, saw education as the key to empowerment and actively promoted it. Shri Ram Avatar and Shri Govind Paswan, her dedicated teachers, went beyond the call of duty to provide and support her with money and means other than the quality education, employing innovative teaching methods that made even the most complex subjects accessible. She also mentioned her dear friend Mahesh, whose parallel journey constantly inspired her to strive for excellence.

When Prakash asked about the specific ways Mukhiya Jee and her teachers influenced her educational journey, Sujata's eyes sparkled with fond memories. Mukhiya Jee, she explained, was more than a leader; he was a hope in their community. He organized study groups and convinced parents of the importance of schooling. His own daughters were among the first to receive formal education, setting a powerful example. Shri Ram Avatar and Shri Govind Paswan, she continued, were relentless in their commitment to education. Shri Ram Avatar was known for his creative teaching strategies, while Shri Govind Paswan, through personal sacrifices, ensured they had the best resources available. Their efforts instilled in her a deep love for learning and the confidence to dream beyond the confines of their village.

Pramila then probed into the challenges Sujata faced during her studies. Sujata recounted the myriad obstacles with a blend of humility and determination. Financial constraints were a constant struggle, as were societal pressures that dictated a girl's place was at home and education to her community was just denied. She painted a poignant image of evenings spent under the dim glow of a kerosene lamp, juggling household chores with her studies. Overcoming these societal norms required immense perseverance, but the unwavering support from her mentors and family made it possible.

When the topic shifted to her commitment to her community, Sujata's face lit up with pride. She described the genesis of an open sky school and later a small school in their village, a project born from the realization that education was the bedrock of any progressive community.

With the unwavering support of Mukhiya Jee, Shri Ram Avatar, and Shri Govind Paswan, they started this school in a modest, makeshift classroom. Despite numerous challenges, including securing funds and convincing parents to send their children, especially girls, to school, they persevered. Today, that school stands tall, an indication to their collective efforts, providing quality education and symbolizing hope and progress.

Prakash then asked about her preparation for the civil services examination, known for its daunting difficulty. Sujata explained that preparing for this exam required a strategic approach and unwavering dedication. She and Mahesh decided to prepare together, which proved to be a blessing. Their days were meticulously planned, starting early in the morning and stretching late into the night. They broke down the syllabus into manageable parts and focused on understanding concepts rather than rote learning. Regular discussions and mock tests were integral to their preparation. The support from their mentors was invaluable, providing guidance and study materials. Mukhiya Jee ensured they had a conducive environment for study, creating a collective effort that led to her success.

Finally, Pramila asked Sujata for a message to young aspirants, especially those from underrepresented communities. Sujata's voice took on a tone of earnest sincerity as she addressed them. She urged them to believe in themselves and the transformative power of education. "Your circumstances do not define your destiny; your determination does," she asserted. She encouraged young people to surround themselves with supportive individuals who believe in their dreams. Education, she emphasized, is the key that unlocks countless doors, and with hard work and perseverance, anything is achievable.

To those from underrepresented communities, Sujata offered a message of empowerment. "Your background is not a barrier but a unique perspective that can drive meaningful change," she said. She advised them to use their experiences to fuel their ambitions and never let societal norms dictate their potential. Finding mentors, as she did with Mukhiya Jee, Shri Ram Avatar, and Shri Govind Paswan, was crucial. Finally, she stressed the importance of giving back to one's community, as true progress is achieved through collective effort.

The interview concluded with Prakash expressing admiration for Sujata's journey. He wished her continued success in her role as Chief District Officer and looked forward to the positive changes she would bring. Sujata thanked them, hoping her story would inspire others to pursue their dreams and contribute to society.

In the warm light of the afternoon, as Prakash and Pramila left her office, they carried with them not just a story of personal triumph but a narrative of hope, resilience, and the enduring power of education. Ms. Sujata's journey from a small village to becoming a pivotal figure in her district was more than an individual success; it was a stimulus for many young dreamers across the nation. Her tale, filled with challenges and triumphs, stood as a testament to the impact of community support, the importance of education, and the unyielding spirit of determination.

In a world where the narrative of success often follows a linear path of privilege and opportunity, the story of Ms. Sujata stands as a poignant counterpoint. Her journey, captured in the recent interview by Prakash Kumar Ghimire from The Rising Sun and Pramila Shrestha from Gorkha Patra, offers more than a simple tale of perseverance. It is a rich philosophy, historical context, contemporary societal norms, and deeply personal experiences.

From the outset, Sujata's early life in a small village underlines a fundamental philosophical truth: greatness can emerge from the humblest beginnings. Aristotle's concept of eudaimonia—the idea of flourishing through virtue and purpose—resonates deeply with her story. Born into an underprivileged family, Sujata's path was fraught with obstacles that seemed insurmountable. Yet, it was this very adversity that forged her character and resilience. Her journey aligns with the philosophical teachings of Stoicism, particularly the works of Epictetus, who emphasized the strength derived from enduring hardships.

Sujata's ascent was not merely an act of individual will but a testament to the transformative power of education, echoing the sentiments of historical figures, who championed the right to learn even in the face of immense danger. Sujata's narrative also brings to mind the struggle of Sojourner Truth, whose life as an African American abolitionist and women's rights activist in the 19th century United States parallels Sujata's fight against societal norms and gender biases.

Her personal history adds another layer of depth to her story. Widowed in childhood, Sujata faced a cultural stigma that could have easily consigned her to a life of obscurity and subjugation. The early loss of her husband—a man she barely had the chance to know—cast a long shadow over her formative years. Yet, it was within this shadow that Sujata found her strength. Her love for Mahesh, a friend and confidant, provided her with a semblance of normalcy and emotional support. This relationship, though platonic, was steeped in mutual respect and shared aspirations. It was Mahesh who stood by her, studying late into the night, and offering words of encouragement that became the lifeline she desperately needed.

The story of Sujata's triumphs is not merely a catalogue of achievements but a reflection of her indomitable spirit. Her success in the civil services examination, against all odds, is reminiscent of the triumphs of figures like Nelson Mandela, who rose from the ashes of apartheid to lead his nation. Like Mandela, Sujata's journey was marked by a relentless pursuit of justice and equality, driven by an unwavering commitment to her community.

In contemporary society, Sujata's story challenges the often-myopic view of success as a product of inherent privilege. It serves as a powerful reminder that true achievement is often born from struggle and sacrifice. Her efforts to uplift her community, particularly through the establishment of a school, resonate with the educational reforms of figures like Maria Montessori, who believed in the transformative power of learning environments tailored to the needs of the community.

Sujata's feelings, as revealed in the interview, are a complex blend of pride, humility, and a deep sense of responsibility. She speaks of her mentors—Mukhiya Jee, Shri Ram Avatar, and Shri Govind Paswan—with reverence, acknowledging their pivotal roles in her journey. Her love for Mahesh, though not overtly romantic, is a substantiation to the profound impact of companionship and support in overcoming life's adversities.

The philosophical underpinnings of her story are clear: her life embodies the principles of resilience, the pursuit of knowledge, and the importance of community support. Her triumphs are not hers alone but are shared with the countless individuals who believed in her potential and supported her dreams.

In the broader context of history and contemporary society, Sujata's narrative challenges us to reconsider our definitions of success and leadership. Her story illuminates the path for others who, like her, come from humble beginnings but dream of making a significant impact on their world. It is a confirmation to the enduring truth that with determination, support, and a commitment to learning, the barriers imposed by society and circumstance can be transcended.

While understanding Sujata's life, it is vibrant that her journey was not just an individual success story but a profound commentary on the human condition. It underscores the idea that true greatness is often forged in the crucible of adversity and that the measure of a person's success is not where they start, but how they rise.

In a time when borders were mere whispers in the winds, there stood a grand old tree known as Puttalli Gacch, its roots entwined with the rich soils of both India and Nepal. It towered majestically, its ancient limbs a testament to the eons it had witnessed, a silent guardian of the lands it bridged. Beneath its sprawling canopy, the lives of many had unfolded, but none so intimately as that of a young girl named Sujata.

Sujata found serenity in the shadow of Puttalli Gacch, her heart and mind seeking the wisdom that only time and nature could bestow. To her, the tree was not merely a physical entity but a wise mentor, a sage wrapped in a cloak of leaves. The rustle of its branches was the language of the ancients, a dialect understood only by those who listened with their soul.

The tree had stood long before Sujata's ancestors were born, witnessing the rise and fall of empires, the migrations of people, and the silent, steady flow of the river that meandered nearby. Its bark bore the scars of countless seasons, each ring within its core a chapter in the story of the earth itself. It was under this tree that Sujata often sat, her back against its sturdy trunk, feeling the pulse of life that surged within it, a heartbeat that echoed her own.

One summer evening, as the sun began to dip below the horizon, casting a gilded shade over the terrestrial, Sujata approached Puttalli Gacch with a heavy heart. She was torn between the traditions of her heritage and the promise of a future beyond the familiar hills and valleys. As she pressed her palm against the rough bark, she felt a surge of understanding flow through her. The tree seemed to whisper to her in the gentle breeze, its leaves swishing a soothing melody of reassurance.

"Do not fear the unknown," the tree seemed to say, "for I have seen many journeys begin and end. The roots you plant today will nourish you tomorrow. Just as I stand firm with my roots deep in the earth, so too can you find strength in the foundation of your ancestors while reaching for the sky."

Sujata closed her eyes, letting the wisdom of Puttalli Gacch seep into her being. She envisioned the countless generations that had found shade beneath its branches, each one contributing to the life that the tree had beheld. She saw herself, unique yet interconnected, her path guided by the breathes of those who came before her.

With renewed clarity, Sujata opened her eyes and gazed up at the vast expanse of branches above. The leaves fluttered gently, like a thousand tiny hands waving in encouragement. She realized that her journey was not just her own, but part of a larger, timeless dance. The tree, her mentor, had taught her that true wisdom lay not in the fear of the unknown, but in the courage to encompass it.

And so, with the blessings of Puttalli Gacch, Sujata set forth on her path, carrying with her the lessons of the ages. The tree watched over her, its presence a constant reminder of the strength and sturdiness that lay within. As the years passed, Sujata returned often to her beloved tree, each visit a pilgrimage of gratitude and reflection.

In the end, Puttalli Gacch stood as it always had, a custodian of time and of wisdom. Its branches reached out to the heavens, its roots delved deep into the earth, and in its shade, the spirit of Sujata thrived, forever intertwined with the timeless legacy of the grand old tree that knew no borders.

25

"Echoes Of Change: The Transformative Journey Of Sujata And Mahesh"

The story of Sujata and Mahesh, both serving as Chief District Officers in the districts of Malanga and Dhanushka respectively, is one of remarkable dedication, profound love, and transformative social change. Their journey together began in the humble confines of their village, and their shared vision for a better society continued to guide them in their professional roles, even as they worked miles apart.

Sujata, who was once known as Inara Wali, carried her early experiences and challenges with her into her role as CDO of Malanga. Drawing inspiration from ancient philosophical texts and historical precedents, she sought to bring about social justice. Echoing the teachings of Mahatma Gandhi on social equality and the Buddhist principles of compassion and fairness, she implemented programmes aimed at reducing caste-based discrimination. She introduced policies that mandated equal access to public resources and services for all, regardless of caste or economic status.

In the ambit of education, Sujata was inspired by the historical reforms of King Janak of Mithila, who is famed for his progressive views on women's education. She worked tirelessly to improve the educational infrastructure, ensuring that schools were accessible to girls and boys alike. Scholarships were provided to children from underprivileged backgrounds, reflecting the ancient Vedic principle of Vidya Dadati Vinayam – knowledge bestows humility and progress.

Mahesh, stationed in Dhanushka, focused on improving sanitation and health facilities, areas that had long been neglected. Inspired by the public health advancements during the reign of Ashoka the Great, Mahesh implemented comprehensive sanitation programmes. Public latrines were constructed, and existing ones were refurbished. He organized community clean-up drives and educational campaigns on hygiene practices, emphasizing the importance of cleanliness as taught in the Ayurvedic texts.

Health facilities in Dhanushka saw a significant transformation under Mahesh's leadership. Drawing from Florence Nightingale's pioneering work in modern nursing, he established health camps in remote areas, providing medical check-ups and distributing free medicines. Mobile health units were introduced to ensure that even the most isolated communities received medical care. The district hospital was upgraded with better facilities and more staff, aiming to reduce maternal and infant mortality rates, reflecting the compassion inherent in Buddhist teachings.

Access to clean water was another critical area where Sujata and Mahesh made substantial improvements. Inspired by ancient systems of water management like those seen in the Indus Valley Civilization, they undertook extensive projects to build and restore wells and reservoirs. Rainwater harvesting systems were introduced, and public awareness campaigns educated communities about the importance of conserving water.

In terms of food security, Sujata looked back at the agricultural reforms of the ancient Lichhavi dynasty. She initiated programs to support farmers with better seeds, tools, and training in sustainable farming practices. Cooperative societies were formed to help farmers sell their produce at fair prices, ensuring food security and economic stability.

Mahesh, meanwhile, established community kitchens and food distribution centres, inspired by the traditional langar system seen in Sikhism, where food is freely shared with all. These centres ensured that no one in Dhanushka went hungry. Clothing drives were organized, and partnerships with NGOs helped distribute clothes to those in need, providing dignity and warmth to the impoverished.

Above all, both Sujata and Mahesh worked to restore social dignity to the marginalized communities. They created forums where people could voice their grievances and seek justice without fear of retribution. Inspired by the Panchayat system of local self-government, they empowered local communities to take part in decision-making processes.

Their efforts also included celebrating cultural festivals and traditions that promoted unity and respect among diverse communities. This cultural revival was reminiscent of the Chhath Puja, a festival that transcends caste and community lines, promoting harmony and mutual respect.

Despite the physical distance between them, Sujata and Mahesh's bond grew stronger. Their love was a quiet, resilient force that provided them with the emotional strength to face their daily challenges. They wrote letters to each other, filled with encouragement and detailed accounts of their work. These letters were not just about their love but also about their shared vision for the future.

Their love story was reminiscent of the ancient epic tales of love and sacrifice, such as that of Savitri and Satyavan. They found solace in knowing that they were working towards the same goals, even if they were apart. Their connection was a testament to the timeless nature of true love, which flourishes despite adversity and distance.

The impact of Sujata and Mahesh's work was profoundly felt in their home village. The community, which had once struggled under the weight of poverty and social discrimination, began to thrive. The schools that Sujata helped establish produced a generation of educated young people who aspired to continue the cycle of positive change. The health and sanitation improvements initiated by Mahesh led to a significant decline in disease and mortality rates, creating a healthier, more vibrant community.

The villagers spoke with reverence about the changes brought by their once humble neighbours. Elders in the village often recounted the transformation with a sense of pride, noting how the efforts of Sujata and Mahesh had restored not just physical infrastructure, but also the spirit of the community. The sense of social dignity and equality fostered by their programs was perhaps the most significant change, creating a new social fabric where everyone, regardless of caste or economic status, felt valued and respected.

The narrative of Sujata and Mahesh as Chief District Officers is more than a story of professional success. It is a profound tale of social justice, buoyancy, and love. Their efforts in sanitation, health, education, and social dignity, guided by ancient wisdom and contemporary necessity, transformed their districts and inspired a generation. Their enduring love, sustained through distance and dedication, added a deeply human dimension to their professional achievements. The legacy they left stood as a power of vision, hard work, and the unyielding pursuit of a just and equitable society.

26

A Weekend Of Reflections And Resolutions

Mahesh's arrival in Malanga was met with a warm and quiet anticipation. Mahesh chose to pay a visit to Sujata in her office. The weekend, rare in its offering of time together, was a much-needed respite from their rigorous schedules as Chief District Officers. As Mahesh entered Sujata's office, the room filled with the subtle comfort of familiarity and shared history. The simplicity of their presence together spoke volumes, far more than words could capture.

They began their conversation with the mundane – updates on their respective districts, the progress of various initiatives, and the challenges they faced. But as the afternoon light softened, so did their topics of discussion, moving into deeper, more personal territory.

"Sujata," Mahesh began, his voice tinged with both hope and uncertainty, "we've been friends and comrades for so long, and our shared dreams have brought us to this point. But what about us? What does the future hold for you and me, together?"

Sujata looked at him, her eyes reflecting a mix of affection and sorrow. "Mahesh, you know how deeply I care for you. Our bond is something I cherish beyond words. But my path has always been different. The weight of my responsibilities, the expectations of my role...they've shaped me in ways that make the thought of marriage difficult."

Mahesh leaned forward, his expression earnest. "But we've overcome so much together. We've broken barriers and defied odds. Why should this be any different? I believe in us, Sujata. I believe in our ability to carve out a future despite these challenges."

Sujata sighed softly; the sound filled with the incumbrance of her internal conflict. "It's not about our ability, Mahesh. It's about the nature of my commitment. Since I was widowed as a child, my life has been a series of battles against societal norms and personal limitations. Marriage, for me, is not just a union but a symbol of the freedom I've fought so hard to claim. I fear that stepping into that role might tether me in ways I cannot afford."

Her words slung in the air, heavy with unspoken fears and unresolved quandaries. Mahesh sat back, processing the depth of her feelings. He knew her journey intimately – the struggles, the victories, and the sacrifices. He respected her perspective, even as his heart ached for a different answer.

"I understand, Sujata," he said quietly. "But know this – my love and respect for you transcend any traditional definitions of relationships. Whether we marry or not, what we have will always be sacred to me. Our friendship and our shared mission will remain the keystone of my life."

Sujata smiled, her eyes glistening with unshed tears. "That means more to me than you can imagine, Mahesh. You've always been my anchor, my confidant. Our connection is beyond labels, beyond societal conventions. It's something pure and profound."

They sat in silence for a while, each lost in their thoughts. Outside, the world continued its busy pace, but in that office, time seemed to stand still, encapsulating their emotions and reflections.

As the conversation resumed, it took on a more philosophical tone. Sujata spoke of the ancient texts she had read, the philosophies that guided her life. "In the Bhagavad Gita, Krishna speaks of the importance of duty and the path of selfless action. My role as a leader is my dharma, and it requires sacrifices that sometimes include personal desires. I draw strength from these teachings."

Mahesh nodded, understanding the depth of her reference. "And in Impassiveness, as Marcus Aurelius wrote, 'The happiness of your life depends upon the quality of your thoughts.' You've cultivated a mindset that prioritizes the greater good, which is admirable. I see now that our paths, though intertwined, must respect our individual journeys."

Their discussion meandered through reflections on societal norms and the evolution of their roles within it. They talked about the progress they had seen in their districts, the impact of their policies on sanitation, health, and education. Sujata mentioned how the community's respect for her had grown, how people no longer saw her as merely Inara Wali but as a leader who had brought tangible change.

Mahesh shared similar stories from Dhanushka, recounting the smiles of children who now had access to clean water and the gratitude of families who benefitted from the health camps. "We've made strides that our ancestors could only dream of. And yet, there's so much more to do. Our work, our impact, must continue to expand."

The conversation then drifted to their visions for the future. "Imagine a Nepal," Sujata mused, "where every child, regardless of their background, has access to quality education. Where health care is not a privilege but a right. Where women and men stand as equals in every sphere of life."

Mahesh's eyes lit up with the shared dream. "And we'll get there, Sujata. One step at a time, one policy at a time. We are the change-makers, the ones who carry the torch of progress. Our legacy will be the foundation for future generations."

As the evening shadows lengthened, their conversation grew quieter, more introspective. The bond between them, fortified by years of shared struggles and triumphs, felt unbreakable. They knew that their paths, while separate in some ways, would always run parallel in their quest for a better society.

Before Mahesh left, they stood by the window, looking out at the bustling life of Malanga. "We'll meet again soon," Mahesh said, his voice filled with a mixture of hope and resignation.

Sujata nodded; her heart full. "Yes, we will. And until then, our work continues. For our people, for our future."

With a final hug, Mahesh departed, leaving Sujata alone in her office. She watched him go, a sense of peace settling over her. Their love, though not conventional, was strong and enduring. It was a love defined by mutual respect, shared goals, and a deep understanding of each other's dreams and sacrifices.

In the days that followed, Sujata threw herself back into her work with renewed vigour. The weekend with Mahesh had given her clarity and strength. She knew that their relationship, as complex and unconventional as it was, would always be a source of support and inspiration.

The changes they had initiated in their districts were already bearing fruit, but there was so much more to be done. Inspired by their discussions, Sujata launched new initiatives aimed at improving women's rights and creating more inclusive economic opportunities. Mahesh, too, continued to push forward with his health and sanitation projects, ensuring that no community was left behind.

The legacy of their efforts was felt deeply in their home village. The elders, who had witnessed the transformation over the years, spoke with pride of the changes brought by Sujata and Mahesh. The once marginalized community now stood as a tribute to what determination, education, and progressive leadership could achieve.

The story of Sujata and Mahesh is not merely one of love and friendship but of enduring commitment to social justice and progress. Their work, inspired by ancient philosophies and driven by contemporary needs, has set a new standard for what leadership can achieve. Their love, though tested by distance and duty, remains a guiding light, illuminating their paths and the lives of those they touch.

In the end, their story is a powerful reminder that true love and leadership transcend personal desires and societal expectations. They are about creating a better world for all, driven by the unwavering belief that change is possible and that each step, no matter how small, brings us closer to the dream of a just and equitable society.

27

Village Evolutionary Shift

Mukhiya Jee, once a robust pillar of his village, now found himself engulfed by the slow march of time. He missed the constant companionship and support of Sujata and Mahesh, whose assistance had once been a cornerstone of his daily life. Yet, he also felt a deep sense of pride and empowerment as he watched them blossom into their roles as Chief District Officers. Under their guidance, Malanga and the neighbouring villages were undergoing a transformation. Social dynamics were shifting, driven by the energy and assertiveness of the younger generation.

In these villages, success stories abounded, serving as examples of inspiration for the youth. Tales of individuals achieving remarkable goals fuelled the collective ambition, contributing significantly to the local economy and altering the dynamics of families and the broader community. The change was intense: nearly every young child was now attending school. Parents from all walks of life recognized the importance of education, ensuring their children not only went to school but also adhered to strict sanitation practices, completed their homework, and maintained good health and hygiene. The children thrived, growing up in an environment that nurtured their potential, while the elderly enjoyed improved facilities and a sense of contentment.

However, amidst this progress, certain archaic ideologies remained stubbornly entrenched, particularly among the older generation. Concepts of supremacy, bloodline, and lineage continued to wield significant influence. These outdated beliefs manifested in the way they treated family members who married outside their lineage, often subjecting these individuals to indignity and exclusion. Women, in particular, bore the brunt of this discrimination, facing verbal and physical abuse that sometimes escalated to tragic extremes, including suicide and honour killings.

This cultural friction precipitated a new kind of crisis. Educated youth, disillusioned by the regressive attitudes of their elders, began to distance themselves from their families and communities. They pursued higher education in distant cities, found jobs far from home, and married and settled away, rarely returning to their ancestral villages. The demographic fabric of the village began to unravel. The exodus of educated young people left a void, creating a shortage of skilled and educated manpower. Schools, once bustling with children, now faced a dearth of students at the entry level, as the village transformed into little more than a transient stopover for ambitious youth who eventually spread their wings and flew away.

Mukhiya Jee and his fellow educators and friends watched these developments with growing concern. They understood the profound implications of this demographic shift. The village, once a close-knit community, now seemed like a ghost town, with only the elderly and unskilled labourers remaining. The vibrancy that had once characterized Malanga was fading, replaced by a sense of desolation and loss.

Reflecting on these changes, Mukhiya Jee often reminisced about the past. He remembered a time when the village was full of life and energy, a time when every child's laughter echoed through the fields and the community thrived on collective effort and mutual support. Now, he saw a stark contrast: abandoned homes, empty classrooms, and an eerie silence that spoke volumes about the village's plight.

Despite the disheartening scenario, Mukhiya Jee remained hopeful. He believed that the solution lay in bridging the generational divide, fostering understanding and acceptance between the old and the new. He knew that it was essential to challenge and eventually change the outdated beliefs that caused so much strife. To this end, he and his friends organized community meetings, bringing together people of all ages to discuss the village's future. They promoted dialogue and encouraged the sharing of ideas, hoping to kindle a spark of unity and progressive thought.

They also sought to engage the youth who had left, reaching out to them through various channels to remind them of their roots and the importance of their heritage. Mukhiya Jee envisioned a future where the village was not just a stepping stone but a home that people were proud to return to, a place where they could contribute to the community's growth and prosperity.

Through inexorable effort, the seeds of change began to take root. Slowly, attitudes started to shift. Some of the older generation began to recognize the value of education and the need for social equality. The stories of those who had suffered because of rigid traditions served as powerful lessons, prompting a re-evaluation of long-held beliefs.

Youth engagement initiatives began to bear fruit as well. Former villagers, now successful professionals, started to return, bringing with them skills, knowledge, and a renewed sense of purpose. They invested in local businesses, supported educational programs, and worked to improve healthcare and sanitation facilities. The village started to breathe again, revitalized by the influx of energy and ideas.

The transformation was gradual but undeniable. Mukhiya Jee, though older and more reflective, found solace in the small victories. He saw the village slowly reawakening, the demographic balance beginning to restore. Schools started to fill with children once more, and the marketplace buzzed with activity. The social fabric was being rewoven, stronger and more inclusive than before.

In his twilight years, Mukhiya Jee could finally see the fruits of his lifelong dedication. The village was not just surviving; it was evolving into a community where old wisdom and new ideas coexisted harmoniously. The journey was far from over, but the direction was clear. Mukhiya Jee and his friends continued their efforts, driven by the belief that every step forward, no matter how small, was a step towards a brighter future for Malanga and its people.

Sujata and Mahesh, two remarkable personalities, assumed the pivotal roles of Chief District Officers (CDOs) in Nepal, each bringing their unique talents and perspectives to the table. Their contributions to the transformative efforts led by Mukhiya Jee were multifaceted, encompassing scientific, social, and philosophical dimensions that resonated deeply with their community.

From a scientific standpoint, Sujata and Mahesh were instrumental in implementing evidence-based policies and programs aimed at addressing the pressing issues facing their district. At the same time, Sujata and Mahesh recognized the importance of addressing social inequalities that hindered the community's growth. They were vocal advocates for gender equality, working tirelessly to dismantle patriarchal norms and empower women and girls. Through targeted interventions, such as women's education programs and economic empowerment initiatives, they sought to break the cycle of poverty and marginalization, fostering a more inclusive society where everyone had equal opportunities to thrive.

Their efforts were not limited to tangible improvements; Sujata and Mahesh also played a crucial role in fostering a culture of dialogue and cooperation within the community. They facilitated community meetings and forums where people from diverse backgrounds could come together to discuss their concerns, share ideas, and collaborate on solutions. By promoting open communication and mutual respect, they laid the foundation for collective action and social cohesion, essential ingredients for sustainable development.

Moreover, Sujata and Mahesh embraced a holistic approach to development that acknowledged the interplay between human welfare and environmental sustainability. They recognized the importance of preserving the natural resources upon which their community depended, advocating for eco-friendly practices and conservation efforts that safeguarded the local ecosystem for future generations.

In the face of challenges and setbacks, Sujata and Mahesh remained persistent in their commitment to effecting positive change. They approached obstacles as opportunities for growth and learning, drawing upon their resilience and creativity to overcome barriers and find innovative solutions. Their leadership inspired others to join in the collective endeavour of building a brighter future for their community, catalysing a wave of grassroots activism and civic engagement that breathed new life into Malanga and its surrounding villages.

Sujata and Mahesh's contributions as Chief District Officers were instrumental in driving the social, economic, and cultural transformation of their district. Through their scientific acumen, social advocacy, and philosophical outlook, they embodied the spirit of progressive change, leaving an indelible mark on of their community.

28

Nandini & Suman: Their Plight And Influence

Nandini and Suman found solace in their daily rituals at the old stone well at the heart of their village. The well, with its time-worn edges and cool, clear water, became an asylum for their companionship. They meticulously coordinated their schedules to ensure that their paths crossed at least twice each day, a sacred routine that outdid the mundane task of fetching water. The rhythmic creak of the pulley, the splash of the bucket dipping into the depths, and the ensuing chatter became the soundtrack of their mornings and evenings.

But their connection went beyond these essential meetings. Nandini and Suman also arranged a specific hour to converge for other domestic chores, such as washing clothes by the stream. This shared time became a cherished ritual, where they could linger and talk, their voices mingling with the gentle murmur of flowing water and the rustle of leaves in the breeze.

In these precious moments, they peeled back the layers of their daily lives, revealing the trials and tribulations they faced within their homes. The well became more than just a source of water; it was a wellspring of empathy and understanding. They spoke of their families with a mixture of love and lament, sharing stories of harsh words and tender moments, of expectations and disappointments.

Nandini's eyes would often mist over as she recounted the unending demands placed upon her by her in-laws, while Suman's laughter would ring out, defiant and bright, as she narrated her latest rebellion against the unjust restrictions imposed by her family. Together, they forged an unspoken pact of pliability and solidarity, drawing strength from each other's courage and fortitude.

Their meetings were enduring power of female friendship, a light in the oppressive darkness of their domestic lives. The well, the stream, and the simple acts of fetching water and washing clothes became symbols of their shared journey, a journey marked by both hardship and hope. Through their conversations, Nandini and Suman discovered a profound sense of liberation, knowing that in each other, they had found a steadfast ally in the face of life's adversities.

The sun had just begun its drop, casting stretched, golden shadows across the village as Nandini and Suman met by the old well. The well, a symbol of life-giving water and assumed secrets, had become their haven. As they lowered their buckets in unison, the familiar creak of the pulley seemed to echo their shared burdens.

Nandini, her face a mask of quiet determination, broke the silence. "Suman, I cannot bear it any longer. The way they treat us, as though we are outsiders, unworthy of even their basic kindness. My heart aches with the weight of it."

Suman nodded, her eyes flashing with a mixture of sorrow and resolve. "I know, Nandini. Each day feels like an eternity. To be denied participation in household affairs, to be excluded from common prayers—it's as if we are invisible, mere shadows in our own homes. The isolation is unbearable."

They sat on the well's stone edge, their hands busy with the mundane task of drawing water, but their minds racing with thoughts of escape. Nandini spoke softly, almost as if afraid the wind might carry her words to unwanted ears. "Do you remember Madam Sujata, the CDO in Malanga? I've heard she helps women like us, those who are trapped and voiceless. Maybe, just maybe, she could help us find a way out." They already knew that the CDO had gone to Janakpur Zonal Office for a week.

Suman's eyes widened with a flicker of hope. "Yes, I've heard of her. They say she has a kind heart and a strong will. But Nandini, the journey to Janakpur is long and fraught with dangers. And if we are caught..."

Nandini grasped Suman's hand, her grip firm. "We cannot live like this any longer, Suman. To be treated with such disdain, fed from separate utensils because we do not share their blood—it's inhumane. We deserve better than this. Our husbands are away, working hard in Janakpur, oblivious to our suffering. We must take this chance. We must be brave."

Suman looked into Nandini's eyes, seeing the strength she needed mirrored there. "You're right, Nandini. We have to do something. Staying here will only break our spirits further. But how do we leave without raising suspicion?"

Nandini thought for a moment, then spoke with a newfound resolve. "We'll leave in the dead of night, when everyone is asleep. We can take the back roads to avoid detection. I've been saving a little money from the chores I do for the neighbours. It's not much, but it might be enough to get us to Janakpur."

Suman nodded, a plan forming in her mind. "I'll do the same. We'll pack only what we need, enough to sustain us for the journey. We'll move swiftly and silently. And once we reach Janakpur, we'll go straight to Madam Sujata."

The sun dipped below the horizon, casting a gentle twilight over the village. The two women stood; their resolve as unyielding as the ancient stones beneath their feet. They finished their task in silence, their minds already on the path ahead.

As they walked back to their respective homes, Suman turned to Nandini one last time. "Tomorrow night, then. We'll meet here and begin our journey."

Nandini nodded, a faint smile playing on her lips. "Tomorrow night."

The next day passed in a blur of routine and silent anticipation. Nandini and Suman went about their chores, careful not to arouse any suspicion. They endured the usual harsh treatment with a quiet grace, their hearts beating with the promise of freedom.

That night, as the village slept under a blanket of stars, Nandini and Suman met at the well. They carried small bundles of food and clothes, their meagre savings tucked safely away. With a final, resolute glance at the only home they had known since their weddings, they slipped into the shadows.

The journey was arduous, the back roads winding and treacherous. But Nandini and Suman pressed on, driven by the hope of a better life. The nights were cold, and the days long, but they found strength in each other. Their whispered conversations kept their spirits high, their laughter a defiant echo against the silence of the night.

After several days of travel, they finally reached Janakpur. The bustling city was a stark contrast to their quiet village. They made their way to the office of Madam Sujata, their hearts pounding with a mix of fear and anticipation.

Madam Sujata, a woman of striking presence and kind eyes, listened intently as Nandini and Suman poured out their story. She nodded, her expression one of understanding and resolve.

"You have shown great courage in coming here," she said, her voice firm yet gentle. "I will help you. You are not alone in this fight."

With Madam Sujata's assistance, Nandini and Suman found a safe haven with their husbands. They were given the support they needed to rebuild their lives, far from the oppressive confines of their in-laws' homes. They discovered new strengths within themselves, their bond of friendship growing even stronger.

Their journey had not been easy, but it had been necessary. In seeking freedom, they had found not only a new beginning but also the unbreakable power of solidarity. Together, they faced the future with hope and determination, knowing that they had reclaimed their dignity and their right to live as equals.

And so, in the heart of Janakpur, amidst the bustling streets and the promise of new opportunities, Nandini and Suman began their new lives with their husbands, their whispered resolve now resounding evidence to their unyielding spirit.

The sun was high in the sky as a large crowd gathered in front of the Office of the Chief District Officer (CDO) in Malanga. The air buzzed with tension and indignation. The villagers, incited by the families of Nandini and Suman, shouted slogans against Madam Sujata, accusing her of undue interference in their community affairs.

At the heart of the crowd stood Prabhakar, a prominent leader known for his influence and his staunch defence of traditional values. His voice boomed above the clamour, directing the crowd's anger. "Down with Sujata! How dare she meddle in our lives! She seeks to destroy our traditions and our families!"

Inside the office, Sujata sat calmly, her demeanour unruffled despite the uproar outside. She knew this confrontation was inevitable. The door to her office opened, and her assistant, a young woman named Rekha, stepped in, her face pale with worry. "Madam, the crowd is growing restless. They are demanding to see you. Prabhakar is leading them."

Sujata nodded, rising from her chair. "Thank you, Rekha. I will address them."

As she stepped outside, the crowd's noise surged, but she held her ground, her presence commanding attention. Prabhakar, spotting her, pushed his way to the front, his face flushed with anger. "Madam Sujata," he began, his tone accusatory, "you have overstepped your bounds. You've taken our daughters-in-law and turned them against us. You are destroying the fabric of our society!"

Sujata's eyes met his, unwavering. "Prabhakar, I understand your concerns, but let us speak calmly. Nandini and Suman came to me seeking help. They were subjected to unjust treatment in their homes. As a public servant, it is my duty to protect and assist those in need, regardless of community lines."

Prabhakar scoffed, his voice rising. "They were our responsibility, and you had no right to interfere! You are not one of us; you cannot understand our ways. By helping them run away, you have dishonoured our families and our traditions."

Sujata's expression softened, but her resolve remained firm. "Traditions should uphold dignity and justice, not perpetuate suffering and discrimination. Nandini and Suman were treated as outsiders within their own homes, denied basic rights and subjected to harsh treatment. They deserve respect and compassion, just as any human being does."

The crowd murmured, some faces showing doubt, others still hardened by anger. Prabhakar, sensing the wavering of his support, pressed on. "You speak of dignity, but you have brought shame upon us. We will not stand for it."

Sujata raised her hand, her voice steady but strong. "Prabhakar, shame lies not in seeking justice, but in denying it. Nandini and Suman's plight is not an isolated incident; it reflects a broader issue within our society. We must strive to create a community where every individual, regardless of their origins, is treated with fairness and respect."

A ripple of uncertainty spread through the crowd. Some began to lower their placards, their faces reflecting a dawning realization. Prabhakar, seeing his influence wane, tried one last argument. "You say you protect, but you are an outsider, enforcing your beliefs upon us."

Sujata stepped closer, her eyes meeting his with an intensity that silenced the murmurs. "I am an outsider by birth, but I am a protector by duty. My role is not to enforce beliefs, but to ensure that justice is served and human dignity is upheld. I respect traditions, but I cannot condone practices that harm and marginalize. We must evolve and embrace compassion over rigidity."

There was a moment of silence, then a voice from the crowd called out. "What about Nandini and Suman? What will become of them?"

Sujata turned to address the speaker. "Nandini and Suman are with their husbands in Janakpur, with my support. Their husbands deserve to know the truth and have the chance to protect their wives. I believe that reuniting them allowed for healing and understanding."

The crowd, now more subdued, began to disperse, their anger replaced by contemplation. Prabhakar stood still, his face a mixture of frustration and grudging respect. "You may have won today, Sujata, but this is not over."

Sujata smiled gently. "Prabhakar, this is not about winning or losing. It is about creating a society where everyone can live with dignity and respect. I hope that in time, you will come to see that."

As the crowd thinned, Sujata returned to her office, her heart heavy but hopeful. She knew that change was never easy, but it was necessary. She had stood her ground for Nandini and Suman, and in doing so, had sown the seeds for a more just and compassionate community.

In the days that followed, the village began to reflect on the events that had transpired. Some resisted the change, clinging to old ways, but many others began to question and discuss, gradually understanding the importance of equality and justice.

Nandini and Suman, reunited with their husbands in Janakpur, found a new beginning. Their journey had not been without its challenges, but they knew they had made the right choice. With the support of Madam Sujata and their husbands, they started to rebuild their lives, hopeful for a future free from the shadows of their past.

And so, in the quiet town of Malanga, a new chapter began to unfold, one where the voices of justice and compassion began to resonate more strongly, guiding the community towards a brighter and more equitable future.

As the evening shadows lengthened, Madam Sujata made her way to the residence of Mukhiya Jee, the respected village head. Her footsteps were steady, yet there was a tangible sense of urgency in her demeanour. The path to Mukhiya Jee's home was familiar, winding through fields that held with the promise of the night. She knew the significance of this meeting; it was not merely a conversation but a pivotal moment that could shape the future of the village.

Upon arriving, Sujata was greeted by Mukhiya Jee's attendant, who escorted her to the courtyard where the venerable leader sat, surrounded by the tranquil ambiance of his garden. Mukhiya Jee, a man of imposing presence with a wise, weathered face, rose to greet her.

"Madam Sujata, it is an honour to have you here," he said, his voice warm but dignified.

Sujata bowed respectfully. "Mukhiya Jee, the honour is mine. I come seeking your counsel and support."

Mukhiya Jee gestured for her to sit, but Sujata remained standing until he offered her a seat with a nod of approval. "Please, make yourself comfortable," he said.

Once seated, Sujata began, her voice measured and respectful. "Mukhiya Jee, I have come to discuss a matter of great importance concerning the welfare of our village women. Recently, two young brides, Nandini and Suman, fled their homes due to severe mistreatment by their in-laws. They sought refuge and assistance, which I provided, helping them to reunite with their husbands in Janakpur."

Mukhiya Jee listened intently, his eyes reflecting a deep concern. "I have heard whispers of their plight. It saddens me to know such injustice exists within our community."

Sujata continued, her tone earnest. "The treatment they endured is not isolated. It highlights a broader issue of domestic violence and discrimination against women, irrespective of caste, creed, or status. Such acts are not only morally reprehensible but also legally unacceptable. I implore you to convene a Village Panchayat Meeting to address this matter. It is imperative that we send a clear message: any form of domestic violence will be dealt with firmly by the law."

Mukhiya Jee nodded slowly, considering her words. "You are right, Madam Sujata. The sanctity of our homes and the dignity of our women must be preserved. Your actions have shown courage and compassion. I will call for a Panchayat Meeting and ensure that this issue is addressed with the seriousness it deserves."

Relief washed over Sujata. "Thank you, Mukhiya Jee. Your support means a great deal. It is only with the collective will of the community that we can bring about meaningful change."

Mukhiya Jee stood, signalling the end of their meeting. "You have my word, Madam Sujata. We will meet tomorrow at sunrise. May our efforts bear fruit for the betterment of all."

Sujata rose, bowing deeply. "I am grateful for your wisdom and guidance. Together, we can foster a more just and compassionate society."

As she departed, paying her respects once more, Sujata felt a renewed sense of hope. The village's most respected figure was on her side, and that meant a great deal.

The following morning, as the first light of dawn painted the sky in hues of gold and rose, the village gathered in the open courtyard for the Panchayat Meeting. The air was thick with anticipation and murmurs of curiosity. Mukhiya Jee took his place at the head of the assembly, his presence commanding respect.

He raised his hand for silence, and the crowd fell quiet. "Brothers and sisters of our village," he began, his voice resonant, "we have gathered here to address a grave matter. Our daughters, Nandini and Suman, were driven to flee their homes due to severe mistreatment. This is not just a family issue; it is a community issue."

The murmurs grew louder, but Mukhiya Jee continued. "We cannot allow such injustices to continue. Domestic violence and discrimination against women are not only against our values but also against the law. Madam Sujata, our esteemed CDO, has brought this to my attention, and I stand with her in declaring that any such acts will be met with firm legal action."

A middle-aged man, Ravi, stood up, his face flushed with anger. "Mukhiya Jee, you speak of law, but these are our traditions! How can an outsider like Madam Sujata understand our ways and impose her will upon us?"

Mukhiya Jee's gaze was steady. "Traditions should evolve to uphold justice and compassion. Our ways should not justify cruelty. Madam Sujata's actions were in defence of human dignity, a value that transcends all boundaries."

Another voice, softer but firm, spoke from the crowd. It was Lakshmi, a young woman with a baby in her arms.

"Mukhiya Jee, I support what you and Madam Sujata are saying. I have seen and experienced the hardships women face. It is time for change."

The crowd fell silent, reflecting on her words. Mukhiya Jee seized the moment. "Lakshmi speaks the truth. We must protect our women, not oppress them. The Panchayat will henceforth ensure that any cases of domestic violence are reported and dealt with justly. We will set up a committee to support victims and educate our community on the importance of respect and equality."

A wave of agreement rippled through the assembly. Ravi, still reluctant, muttered, "But what about our honour, Mukhiya Jee?"

Mukhiya Jee turned to him; his expression resolute. "Our true honour lies in our ability to protect and uplift all members of our community, especially the vulnerable. We must adapt and grow, or we risk being left behind."

The meeting concluded with a renewed commitment to justice and equality. Sujata, standing at the edge of the gathering, felt a deep sense of accomplishment. The journey was far from over, but the first steps had been taken.

As the villagers dispersed, there was a palpable change in the air. Conversations sparked new ideas, and old prejudices began to wane. Mukhiya Jee's leadership, coupled with Sujata's unwavering resolve, had planted the seeds for a more compassionate and just community.

Sujata returned to her office; her heart buoyed by the progress made. She knew there would be challenges ahead, but she was ready. With allies like Mukhiya Jee and the support of the villagers, she was confident that together, they could build a future where every woman could live with dignity and respect.

29

The Escape of Bhola Singh

The dank, oppressive air of the prison cell seemed to pulse with a latent energy as Bhola Singh and his newfound comrades huddled together in the dim light. Tejas, with his sharp, predatory gaze; Munna, his hulking form radiating raw power; and Sudhir, whose cold, calculating eyes betrayed his ruthless nature, formed an unholy alliance with Bhola. Bound by their shared contempt for authority and a thirst for freedom, they plotted their escape with meticulous precision.

Bhola began, his voice a low whisper that cut through the silence. "We've all suffered under this system long enough. It's time we take our fate into our own hands. The plan is simple but requires absolute coordination. We each have a role to play."

Tejas nodded, his eyes gleaming with a murderous intensity. "I've been observing the guards' routines for weeks. There's a window during the night shift when the security is lax. That's our moment."

Munna grunted in agreement. "And I've managed to bribe a few of the weaker guards. They'll turn a blind eye when the time comes. Our biggest challenge will be the perimeter wall."

Sudhir leaned forward, his expression one of cold resolve. "I've procured a set of tools from the workshop. We'll need to dig our way through the weaker section of the wall near the laundry room. It's less patrolled and offers the best chance of success."

The men spent the following nights quietly gathering their resources and refining their plan. They bribed more guards, ensuring the night shift would be in their favour. Tejas sketched out detailed maps of the prison's layout, marking guard posts and surveillance blind spots. Munna secured additional tools and makeshift weapons, while Bhola maintained their cover, ensuring their activities remained unnoticed by the prison authorities.

As the night of their escape approached, a tense anticipation hung in the air. They gathered in their cell one final time to review the plan.

"Remember," Bhola said, his voice steely, "timing is everything. We move as one, no hesitation. Tejas, you lead the way to the laundry room. Munna, you and I will handle the digging. Sudhir, you keep watch and handle any unexpected surprises."

The others nodded, their faces grim and determined. That night, under the cloak of darkness, they made their move. Tejas led them through the labyrinthine corridors of the prison, his every step confident and sure. They reached the laundry room without incident, and Munna quickly set to work on the wall, his powerful blows muffled by the thick prison walls.

Sudhir kept a vigilant watch, his keen eyes scanning the shadows for any sign of movement. Minutes felt like hours as Munna's efforts finally yielded a narrow passage through the wall. One by one, they squeezed through, emerging into the cool night air beyond the prison's confines.

They sprinted across the open ground, their hearts pounding with the thrill of impending freedom. Just as they reached the outer perimeter, an alarm sounded, piercing the night with its shrill cry. The guards, alerted to their escape, mobilized swiftly.

"Run!" Bhola shouted, his voice filled with urgency. They scattered, each heading in a different direction to confuse their pursuers. Tejas vaulted over a low fence, disappearing into the shadows. Munna used his brute strength to force his way through a locked gate, while Sudhir slipped into the dense underbrush bordering the prison grounds.

Bhola led the authorities on a frantic chase through the night. His knowledge of the terrain and his cunning mind allowed him to stay just one step ahead. He darted through narrow alleyways, scaled walls, and blended into the darkness, evading capture at every turn.

Meanwhile, the prison guards, aided by local police, fanned out in a coordinated effort to recapture the fugitives. They set up roadblocks, combed through nearby forests, and questioned locals, but the escaped convicts seemed to vanish like smoke into the night.

Tejas, with his predatory instincts, found refuge in an abandoned warehouse. He stayed low, using his wits to evade the sweeping searchlights and patrols. Munna, with his brute strength and endurance, forged through the wilderness, covering miles each night and resting during the day. Sudhir, ever the calculating mind, took shelter in a network of caves he had scouted months prior, waiting for the initial frenzy to die down.

Days turned into weeks, and the search for Bhola Singh and his companions intensified. The police, driven by the high-profile nature of the escape, left no stone unturned. Yet, despite their best efforts, the fugitives eluded capture, their trails growing colder with each passing day.

Bhola, ever the strategist, contacted each of his allies through covert means, orchestrating a reunion in a secluded hideout far from the prison. They gathered; their faces gaunt but eyes alight with the fire of freedom.

"We did it," Bhola said, his voice a mixture of triumph and exhaustion. "We're free men now, but we must remain vigilant. The world out there is just as dangerous, if not more so, than the prison we left behind."

Tejas grinned, his predatory gaze unwavering. "We've survived this long because we know how to adapt. We'll continue to do so."

Munna and Sudhir nodded, their resolve firm. They knew the road ahead was fraught with peril, but they were prepared to face whatever came their way, united by their shared experiences and an unbreakable bond forged in the crucible of their escape.

As the authorities' efforts dwindled and the media frenzy subsided, Bhola Singh and his companions faded into the shadows, living lives marked by constant vigilance and the ever-present threat of recapture. Their escape became the stuff of legend, a testament to their cunning and indomitable will.

In the annals of the prison, their names were etched in infamy, a stark reminder of the thin line between order and chaos, and the relentless human spirit's quest for freedom, no matter the cost.

The atmosphere in the Jail Superintendent's office was tense, the gravity of the situation weighing heavily on everyone present. Superintendent Shri Mohan Lal sat at the head of a long, polished table, his stern face lined with worry and frustration. To his right, Deputy Warden Rajesh Malhotra shuffled nervously, glancing occasionally at the empty seats as other members of the prison staff filed in. At the far end of the table, Madam Sujata, the Chief District Officer (CDO), sat with an air of calm authority, her sharp eyes missing nothing.

Superintendent Lal began, his voice tight with controlled anger. "Ladies and gentlemen, we are facing a crisis. Bhola Singh and three of the most dangerous inmates have escaped. This incident is not just a blow to our security but a stain on our reputation. We need to understand how this happened and how to rectify it."

Deputy Warden Malhotra, sweating profusely, spoke up. "Sir, we had no indication that an escape of this scale was being planned. Bhola Singh had been presenting himself as a model prisoner. He even helped in maintaining order among the inmates."

Madam Sujata interjected; her tone measured but firm. "Superintendent Lal, we need to dig deeper. Bhola Singh's record shows a pattern of manipulation. His good behaviour was likely a smokescreen. We need to examine the internal dynamics more closely."

Superintendent Lal nodded, turning to Chief Guard Ram Prasad. "What about the guards on duty? How did they fail to notice the escape in progress?"

Ram Prasad, a grizzled veteran with years of service, cleared his throat. "Sir, I believe some guards may have been compromised. There were rumours of bribery, but I didn't think it was this extensive. I take full responsibility for not investigating those leads more thoroughly."

Madam Sujata's eyes narrowed. "Compromised guards? This indicates a deeper corruption within the ranks. We must root this out if we are to restore order and prevent future incidents."

The room fell silent as Superintendent Lal pondered their next steps. He then addressed the group with renewed determination. "We will launch an immediate internal investigation. Every guard on duty that night will be questioned. Rajesh, I want you to lead this effort. No stone must be left unturned."

Deputy Warden Malhotra nodded, eager to redeem himself. "Yes, sir. I will start the interrogations right away."

Madam Sujata leaned forward, her gaze extreme. "In addition to the investigation, we need to strengthen our security protocols. This escape exposed several vulnerabilities that must be addressed. I suggest we install additional surveillance team in the less monitored areas and increase patrol frequency, especially during the night shift."

Superintendent Lal agreed. "Excellent suggestions, Madam Sujata. We must also revisit our inmate evaluation processes. Bhola Singh's ability to deceive us indicates a flaw in our assessment methods. We need psychological profiles that can better detect manipulative behaviour."

Chief Guard Ram Prasad added, "We should also consider rotating guards more frequently. Familiarity breeds complacency and corruption. Fresh eyes can sometimes see what others miss."

As the discussion continued, the focus shifted to the specifics of the escape. Superintendent Lal turned to Ram Prasad once more. "Tell us about the escape route. How did they manage to bypass the security measures?"

Ram Prasad unfolded a map of the prison on the table. "They exploited a weakness near the laundry room. It's less patrolled, and they used tools to dig through a section of the wall. Once outside, they scattered, making it difficult for the response teams to track them."

Madam Sujata frowned. "This indicates they had significant knowledge of the prison layout and guard schedules. We must assume they had inside help."

Superintendent Lal slammed his fist on the table. "This treachery will not go unpunished. We will find the collaborators and ensure they face the full weight of the law."

The meeting continued late into the night, with detailed plans laid out for both the internal investigation and the overhaul of security protocols. As the staff departed, their faces were set with grim determination. Superintendent Lal, Madam Sujata, and the others knew they were facing a monumental task, but they were united in their resolve to restore order and prevent future breaches.

The next morning, the prison was a hive of activity. Interrogations began promptly, with guards being questioned about their whereabouts and actions on the night of the escape. Rajesh Malhotra worked tirelessly, sifting through testimonies, looking for inconsistencies and signs of deceit.

Meanwhile, Madam Sujata coordinated with external contractors to expedite the installation of new surveillance equipment. She also arranged for a team of psychologists to start reassessing inmates, focusing on identifying potential manipulators and instigators.

As days turned into weeks, the investigation uncovered a network of corruption that extended deeper than anyone had anticipated. Several guards were found to have accepted bribes from Bhola Singh and his associates, and disciplinary actions were swiftly taken. The compromised guards were removed from their positions, and criminal charges were filed against them.

Superintendent Lal, despite the mounting pressure, remained steadfast. He worked closely with Madam Sujata to implement the recommended security measures, ensuring that no detail was overlooked. The prison slowly transformed into a fortress of vigilance, with enhanced surveillance and tighter control over inmate activities.

In the midst of these changes, efforts to recapture Bhola Singh and his accomplices intensified. Law enforcement agencies across the region were alerted, and a special task force was established to track down the fugitives. Leads were followed meticulously, and public appeals for information were made.

One evening, as Superintendent Lal and Madam Sujata reviewed the progress of the reforms, an officer burst into the room. "Sir, ma'am, we've received a tip about Bhola Singh's whereabouts. He was spotted near a border town."

Superintendent Lal stood up; his expression resolute. "Mobilize the task force immediately. We cannot let him slip through our fingers again."

As the task force moved into action, the tension in the prison eased slightly. There was a glimmer of hope that the fugitives would soon be back behind bars. However, the lessons learned from the escape and subsequent investigation remained ingrained in the minds of the prison staff.

Months later, Superintendent Lal and Madam Sujata reflected on the incident and its aftermath. "We've made significant progress," Sujata said. "But we must remain vigilant. Bhola Singh's escape exposed weaknesses that we can never afford to ignore again."

Lal nodded. "Agreed. This experience has taught us the importance of constant vigilance and integrity. We must continue to uphold these values to ensure the safety and security of our institution."

The reforms implemented in the wake of Bhola Singh's escape set a new standard for prison security. While the hunt for Bhola and his accomplices continued, the prison staff remained dedicated to their duty, determined to prevent such an incident from ever occurring again.

As the sun rested over the bolstered prison, a renewed sense of order and discipline took hold. The memory of Bhola Singh's escape became a catalyst for change, driving the staff to maintain the highest standards of vigilance and integrity. The prison, once a place of complacency, had transformed into a bastion of security.

The audacious escape of Bhola Singh and his cohort of hardened criminals cast a long shadow over the prison and its environs, igniting a palpable sense of fear and urgency. Particularly vulnerable were Madam Sujata, the Chief District Officer, and Mukhiya Jee, the village head, both of whom had been instrumental in orchestrating the stringent reforms post-escape. Their determined efforts to dismantle the network of corruption and enhance security protocols had not gone unnoticed by Bhola Singh's loyalists, who viewed these actions as direct threats to their influence and operations. As gossips of retaliation grew louder, it became evident that the lives of these two pivotal figures were in grave danger. Recognizing the imminent threat, Superintendent Shri Mohan Lal, in collaboration with law enforcement agencies, implemented a series of comprehensive security measures. Armed escorts were assigned to both Madam Sujata and Mukhiya Jee, ensuring their safety during their daily commutes and public engagements. Surveillance systems were fortified around their residences, with extra men at strategic points to monitor any suspicious activities. Additionally, a dedicated team of undercover officers was deployed to shadow their movements discreetly, ready to intervene at the slightest hint of danger. The local police increased patrols in the vicinity of their homes, creating a visible deterrent against potential attackers. Furthermore, emergency protocols were established, including direct lines of communication to rapid response units, ensuring swift action in case of any threat. Despite these heightened precautions, Madam Sujata and Mukhiya Jee continued their work with undeterred resolve, their unwavering commitment to justice and reform serving as a beacon of hope for the community. The fortified security measures, combined with their indomitable spirit, created a resilient front against the encroaching shadows, reinforcing the message that the pursuit of integrity and safety would not be silenced by fear.

In the hushed shadows of their clandestine hideout, Bhola Singh and his cohorts—Tejas, Munna, and Sudhir—convened under the cover of night, their faces etched with determination and a glimmer of ruthless intent. Having narrowly escaped the clutches of law enforcement, they knew their immediate survival hinged on slipping across the border into anonymity. Disguises were meticulously crafted: Tejas would adopt the guise of a humble traveling merchant, his sharp features softened by a thick beard and rustic attire; Munna, with his imposing frame, would pose as a wandering labourer, his formidable strength concealed beneath layers of ragged clothing; Sudhir, ever the master of deception, transformed into a pious ascetic, his cold, calculating eyes hidden behind the serene mask of a holy man. Bhola, the orchestrator of their escape, would blend seamlessly into the backdrop as a nondescript farmer, his charismatic presence muted by the garb of the common folk.

Their plan was simple yet fraught with peril: to traverse the rugged terrain under the guise of a disparate group of travellers, converging only at predetermined safe houses dotted along the route. Each would travel separately, avoiding main roads and populous towns, communicating through a series of coded messages left at hidden drop points. They aimed to reach a small, inconspicuous border village, known for its labyrinthine alleys and sympathetic residents willing to harbour fugitives for the right price. Once across the border, they would disappear into the teeming masses of a foreign land, biding their time until the fervour of the hunt for them waned.

Their ultimate goal was not mere survival but a strategic retreat to regroup and plan their return with vengeance and precision. Bhola envisioned a future where they would strike back at those who had dared to imprison them, their actions calculated to sow fear and reclaim their power. As they prepared to embark on their perilous journey, each man harboured his own thoughts and ambitions, yet they were united by a shared resolve to outwit the forces arrayed against them. With final affirmations and a sense of grim determination, they set off into the night, each step taking them closer to the promise of temporary sanctuary and the opportunity to rewrite their fates.

Puttalli Gacch, an ancient tree, stood at the edge of the village, its gnarled roots inscrutable in the soil of history and its branches whispering secrets to the wind. For centuries, it had seen the ebb and flow of human lives, the joys of harvests and the sorrows of famine, the quietude of peace and the tumult of conflict. Now, as the moon cast a silvery glow upon its leaves, the tree sensed a disturbance in the fabric of its world.

The night was unusually silent, the air heavy with the scent of impending change. Puttalli Gacch felt the tremors of restless souls beneath its branches—the hurried, clandestine movements of Bhola Singh and his men. The tree's ancient heart, a vast network of interwoven memories and emotions, resonated with a deep, melancholic understanding of their plight. It could feel their fear, their desperation, and the dark thrill of their audacious escape.

As Bhola Singh and his friends moved stealthily in their disguises, Puttalli Gacch extended its silent blessing, its leaves rustling softly in the gentle night breeze. The tree had seen many such nights, where men sought refuge in its shadows, their fates intertwined with its own enduring presence. It bore witness to their whispered plans and felt the weight of their resolve, each step they took resonating through its roots like the drumbeats of an ancient, unending symphony of survival and resistance.

The tree remembered when it was a mere sapling, standing witness to other fugitives, other desperate escapes. It had provided shelter to rebels, lovers, and wanderers alike, all seeking solace in its enduring strength. Tonight was no different. Bhola, Tejas, Munna, and Sudhir were but the latest in a long line of souls seeking the sanctuary of its silent, watchful presence.

Puttalli Gacch, though firmly rooted in the earth, felt an empathetic connection to their journey. It understood the need for disguise, the desire to evade the relentless pursuit of justice, the yearning for a moment's respite in a world that seemed unforgiving. As the men moved closer to the border, the tree extended its silent wishes for their safe passage, its branches gently swaying as if to guide them on their perilous path.

In its solitude, the tree pondered the cyclical nature of existence. It had outlived generations, bearing witness to countless tales of courage and cowardice, triumph and tragedy. Yet, for all the human drama that unfolded beneath its boughs, Puttalli Gacch remained a steadfast symbol of endurance and resilience. It stood as a silent testament to the passage of time, a living repository of the village's collective memory.

As dawn approached and the fugitives moved further away, Puttalli Gacch felt a profound sense of sorrow and hope intertwined. It mourned the loss of innocence and the harsh realities that drove men to such desperate measures, yet it also harboured a flicker of hope for their redemption and return. The tree, rooted deeply in the soil and the soul of the land, would continue to stand as a silent guardian, its ancient limbs reaching out to embrace the future, whatever it might hold.

In the gentle light of the rising sun, Puttalli Gacch stood tall and resolute, its leaves shimmering with dew and silent wisdom. It would remember this night, as it remembered all the nights before, and it would stand ready to offer its quiet solace to all who sought its shelter, a timeless witness to the enduring human spirit.

30

The Decision Of Heart And Mind

The evening air was cool and fragrant as Mahesh approached the grand old house of Mukhiya Jee, feeling a mixture of nervousness and determination. Baldev Lal Das, Mukhiya Jee's elder son and a renowned professor at a prestigious Indian university, was home. Mahesh had always admired Baldev for his wisdom and progressive views, making him the ideal confidant for his delicate mission.

After initial pleasantries and catching up, Mahesh found a moment alone with Baldev in the courtyard, the soft murmur of evening prayers providing a serene backdrop. Gathering his courage, he began to speak.

"Baldev Jee, I have come with a matter close to my heart. Sujata and I... our bond is deep, and I wish to marry her. But I know this is not a decision I can make alone. I seek your guidance and support."

Baldev looked at Mahesh thoughtfully, his eyes reflecting both curiosity and concern. "Mahesh, you speak of a union that is not just personal but carries significant societal implications. Sujata, once known as Inara Wali, has risen to a position of great responsibility and respect. This is not a decision to be taken lightly."

Mahesh nodded; his resolve unwavering. "I understand, Baldev Jee. But my love for Sujata is profound and genuine. Our shared goals and visions only strengthen my desire to spend my life with her."

Baldev sighed, recognizing the sincerity in Mahesh's voice. "Let us speak to Mukhiya Jee. He holds the family's legacy and societal standing in his hands. His blessing is paramount."

Together, they walked into the inner chamber where Mukhiya Jee sat in quiet contemplation. The flickering lamp cast long shadows on the walls, creating an atmosphere of gravitas and tradition. Baldev, ever respectful, bowed slightly before speaking.

"Father, Mahesh has something important to discuss with you. It concerns his future and the future of our community."

Mukhiya Jee looked up, his wise eyes narrowing slightly. "Speak, Mahesh. What weighs on your heart?"

Taking a deep breath, Mahesh began, "Mukhiya Jee, I wish to marry Sujata. Our journey together has been one of mutual respect and shared dreams. I believe that together, we can continue to bring positive changes to our society."

Mukhiya Jee listened intently; his expression unreadable. After a moment, he spoke, his voice steady and deliberate. "Mahesh, your request is bold. Sujata, though once a simple village girl, has now become a symbol of progress and change. Marrying her is not just a personal decision but a statement to society. Have you considered the ramifications?"

Baldev interjected gently, "Father, times are changing. Our lineage is strong and resilient, but we must also adapt to new realities. Mahesh and Sujata together can set a powerful example, merging tradition with progress."

Mukhiya Jee's gaze shifted to his son, then back to Mahesh. "Family lineage is not just about bloodlines, Mahesh. It is about upholding values, traditions, and the respect we command in society. Sujata's rise is commendable, but marriage brings with it expectations and scrutiny."

Mahesh replied with quiet conviction, "Mukhiya Jee, our lineage is indeed our pride, but progress and change are also vital. Sujata embodies both the strength of tradition and the spirit of progress. Together, we can honour our heritage while forging a new path for the future."

Mukhiya Jee's expression softened slightly as he leaned back, contemplating the young man's words. "Philosophy teaches us the importance of balance, Mahesh. The Bhagavad Gita speaks of duty and the path of righteousness. Our duties to family, society, and self must be harmonized. Do you believe you and Sujata can maintain this balance?"

Mahesh nodded firmly. "Yes, Mukhiya Jee. We have faced many challenges together, and our commitment to each other and to our duties has only strengthened. Our union can bring harmony and inspire others to look beyond rigid conventions."

Baldev added, "Father, consider the teachings of Raja Janak, a king known for his wisdom and progressive thinking. He saw beyond societal norms to the greater good. In supporting Mahesh and Sujata, we honour our past while embracing the future."

Mukhiya Jee closed his eyes, lost in thought. The room fell silent, the only sound the distant rustling of leaves and the occasional chirp of a night bird. When he finally spoke, his voice was reflective.

"Divinity, too, teaches us compassion and understanding. Our gods and ancestors have shown us that love and respect transcend societal boundaries. If Mahesh and Sujata's union can bring greater good and uphold the values we cherish, then it is a path worth considering."

He looked directly at Mahesh, his gaze piercing yet kind. "You have my tentative blessing, Mahesh. But remember, this union will be watched by many. It must be an ideal of hope, integrity, and progress. Do not take this responsibility lightly."

Mahesh bowed deeply, gratitude and determination shining in his eyes. "Thank you, Mukhiya Jee. I promise to honour this trust and work tirelessly to uphold the values and responsibilities that come with it."

As they left the room, Baldev placed a reassuring hand on Mahesh's shoulder. "You have taken a significant step today, Mahesh. The road ahead will not be easy, but with determination and mutual respect, you and Sujata can overcome any obstacle."

Outside, the night air was cool and filled with the scent of blooming jasmine. Mahesh felt a sense of peace and purpose. The discussion with Mukhiya Jee had been challenging, but it had also solidified his resolve. He knew that with Baldev's support and Mukhiya Jee's blessing, albeit cautious, he and Sujata could face the future with confidence.

The conversation had not just been about their marriage; it had been a reflection on the evolving nature of society. It highlighted the delicate balance between tradition and progress, between duty and personal desires. It was a microcosm of the broader changes that Mahesh and Sujata were striving to bring about in their respective roles.

In the days that followed, Mahesh and Sujata continued their work with renewed vigour. Their love, now tempered by the understanding and support of their elders, felt stronger and more resilient. They knew that their path was not just about personal happiness but about setting an example for others.

Their story, marked by philosophical reflections and societal implications, became an optimism for many. It showed that love and duty, tradition and progress, could coexist harmoniously. It was a testament to the power of understanding, respect, and the courage to challenge and redefine societal norms.

As Mahesh returned to Dhanushka, he carried with him the weight of responsibility and the lightness of hope. The discussions with Baldev and Mukhiya Jee had been pivotal, guiding him and Sujata toward a future where their union could inspire and lead.

Together, they continued to work towards a society that respected tradition but embraced progress, a society where love and duty walked hand in hand, forging a path of hope, equality, and justice for all.

The sun was beginning to set as Mukhiya Jee and Baldev arrived at Sujata's office in Malanga. The air was filled with the fragrance of blooming flowers, a soft reminder of the village they all cherished. Sujata, once Inara Wali, now Chief District Officer, welcomed them with grace and a quiet dignity that bespoke her journey from the village to a position of significant authority.

As they settled into her office, the atmosphere was charged with both anticipation and solemnity. Mukhiya Jee, his stature imposing yet softened by age and wisdom, began the conversation with measured tones.

"Sujata," he said, his voice steady but placid, "we have come to discuss something that has been on our minds and hearts. Mahesh, as you know, has expressed his desire to tie the knot with you. We have thought deeply about this and wanted to hear your thoughts directly."

Sujata's eyes met Mukhiya Jee's, reflecting both respect and the weight of her own internal conflict. She knew this conversation would be pivotal, not just for her and Mahesh, but for the larger community that looked up to her.

"Mukhiya Jee, Baldev Bhaiya," she began, her voice calm and clear, "I am honoured by your visit and the consideration you have shown. Mahesh is a dear friend and a remarkable person. Our journey together has been one of mutual respect and shared aspirations. However, marriage is not a decision I can take lightly, given my responsibilities and the principles I hold dear."

Baldev leaned forward; his expression thoughtful. "Sujata, we understand the gravity of your role and the complexities it entails. But marriage can be a source of strength, a partnership that amplifies both personal and professional endeavours. Mahesh's intentions are sincere, and together, you could set a powerful example for others."

Sujata smiled gently, appreciating Baldev's perspective. "Bhaiya, I do not doubt Mahesh's sincerity or his capabilities. He is an exceptional leader and a person of great integrity. But my path is unique. Since childhood, my life has been shaped by the need to rise above societal expectations and to fight for the dignity of those who have been marginalized. Marriage, in many ways, could constrain the freedom I have fought so hard to achieve."

Mukhiya Jee nodded, his eyes reflecting a deep understanding of her struggle. "Your journey, Sujata, has indeed been extraordinary. You have broken barriers and set new standards. But remember, our ancient texts, like the Bhagavad Gita, speak of balance – the importance of duty not only to society but also to oneself and one's family. Can there not be a harmony between your personal desires and your professional responsibilities?"

Sujata's gaze softened as she responded, "Mukhiya Jee, the Bhagavad Gita also teaches us about the importance of one's own path – 'Swadharma.' My path, my 'Swadharma,' has always been to serve my people without any personal ties that might influence my decisions. My commitment is to the greater good, and I fear that entering into marriage might create conflicts between personal and public duties."

Baldev interjected, "Sujata, your dedication to your duties is commendable and inspiring. But consider the support system marriage can provide. A partnership with Mahesh could reinforce your mission rather than hinder it. Together, you can face challenges and continue to drive change."

Sujata's eyes filled with gratitude for Baldev's understanding yet remained resolute. "Bhaiya, I understand your point. But my decision is not just about practicality; it is also deeply philosophical and personal. The teachings of great leaders like Raja Janak, who remained detached despite his royal duties, resonate with me. My detachment allows me to make impartial decisions, free from personal biases or pressures."

Mukhiya Jee, contemplating her words, spoke again, his tone gentle yet firm. "Family lineage and societal respect are significant aspects of our heritage. Marrying Mahesh would not diminish these but could, in fact, strengthen them. Our community would see it as a union of two progressive minds working towards a common goal."

Sujata took a deep breath, her resolve clear. "Mukhiya Jee, I respect our heritage and the values it upholds. However, my commitment to social justice and my role as a CDO demand a level of independence that marriage might compromise. My decisions must remain unaffected by any personal affiliations to ensure fairness and justice for all."

Baldev nodded slowly, seeing the depth of her conviction. "You speak with the wisdom and clarity of a true leader, Sujata. But think also of the companionship and mutual support that marriage can bring. Mahesh respects your vision and shares your goals. Your partnership could be a beacon of progress and modernity."

Sujata's voice softened, reflecting her deep internal struggle. "I do not doubt the potential strength of such a partnership, Bhaiya. But my life has been dedicated to breaking free from the constraints that society has placed on women like me. Marrying Mahesh, despite the respect and love I have for him, might inadvertently bind me in ways that could affect my mission."

Mukhiya Jee, understanding the weight of her words, leaned back, his expression one of acceptance and respect. "Your clarity and commitment are admirable, Sujata. It is evident that your path is guided by a profound sense of duty and purpose. We respect your decision and your dedication to the principles you hold dear."

Sujata's eyes filled with gratitude and relief. "Thank you, Mukhiya Jee, Bhaiya. Your understanding means the world to me. My love and respect for Mahesh will never diminish, but marriage is not the right path for me. My focus remains on serving our people and fulfilling the responsibilities entrusted to me."

The room fell into a reflective silence, each of them contemplating the weight of Sujata's decision and the philosophical and practical considerations that underpinned it. The evening light cast long shadows, symbolizing the complex interplay of tradition, duty, and personal freedom.

After a while, Mukhiya Jee stood up, his face calm and thoughtful. "Sujata, your decision, while difficult, is one that reflects your integrity and dedication. We honour your commitment to your path and will continue to support you in your endeavours."

Baldev also rose, placing a reassuring hand on Sujata's shoulder. "You have our respect and our support, Sujata. Your journey is a testament to the strength of character and the power of self-determination. Continue to lead with the wisdom and courage that have brought you this far."

Sujata smiled, feeling a deep sense of peace and gratitude. "Thank you, Mukhiya Jee, Bhaiya. Your support strengthens my resolve. Together, we will continue to strive for a better society, guided by the values and principles that unite us."

As they left her office, the bond of mutual respect and understanding between them felt stronger than ever. The discussion, though challenging, had reinforced the shared values and goals that bound them. Sujata watched them leave, her heart filled with a sense of purpose and clarity.

In the days that followed, Sujata and Mahesh continued their work with renewed dedication, their shared mission undeterred by the complexities of personal relationships. Their story, now more than ever, stood as the power of commitment to societal progress and the unwavering pursuit of justice.

Their paths, though separate in personal terms, remained intertwined in their collective efforts to bring about meaningful change. The community watched and learned, inspired by their leaders' ability to balance personal sacrifice with public duty, driven by a profound sense of purpose and an unyielding commitment to the greater good.

Thus, Sujata's decision, grounded in philosophical reflection, religious respect, and a deep understanding of societal needs, became another chapter in the ongoing narrative of progress and justice, a blaze for future generations striving to standardise tradition with modernity and personal aspirations with public responsibilities.

Mahesh sat alone in his office in Dhanushka, the dim light of the evening casting a soft glow on the scattered papers and books that lay around him. The decision that had been made weighed heavily on his heart, yet it was a burden he had chosen to bear with grace. Sujata's words echoed in his mind, her resolve to remain unmarried and dedicated to her mission resonating deeply within him. He took a deep breath and began to reflect, allowing his thoughts to form a monologue that would console and guide him through this period of solitude.

"Sujata, your decision, though painful, is one I understand and respect. Love, in its truest form, is about understanding and acceptance. I see now that your path is one of unparalleled dedication and service, a path that requires the freedom to act without personal constraints. How could I, in good conscience, bind you to a life that might detract from your noble mission?"

Mahesh rose from his chair and walked to the window, looking out at the serene landscape bathed in the soft twilight. The tranquillity outside contrasted with the turmoil within, yet he felt a strange sense of peace. "The Bhagavad Gita speaks of 'Nishkama Karma,' the act of performing one's duty without attachment to the results. Sujata's decision embodies this principle perfectly. She has chosen her path, not out of disregard for our love, but out of a higher duty to society. How can I not admire and support her for that?"

He turned away from the window and walked to his desk, picking up a small statue of Lord Krishna. The deity's serene smile seemed to offer solace. "Krishna, you taught Arjuna that true fulfilment comes from duty and righteousness. My duty now is to accept this path with grace and to support Sujata from afar. Our love need not be confined to the bonds of marriage; it can transcend such boundaries and manifest in our shared commitment to justice and progress."

Sitting down again, Mahesh let his thoughts drift to their past, the moments of camaraderie and shared dreams. "Sujata, our journey together has always been one of mutual respect and shared aspirations. We have stood by each other through countless challenges, and though we may not walk the same personal path, our professional and spiritual journeys remain intertwined. In the Upanishads, it is said that the soul is not confined by the body; it is eternal and boundless. Our love, too, is not confined by social constructs. It is eternal, transcending the physical and finding expression in our work."

The room seemed to hum with a quiet energy, as if the universe itself acknowledged his thoughts. Mahesh felt a sense of calm enveloping him, a reassurance that his decision to remain unmarried was the right one. "By choosing not to marry, I honour the purity of our bond and the depth of our shared mission. It is a sacrifice, yes, but one that aligns with the principles I hold dear. Like the sages who sought enlightenment through renunciation, I too seek a higher purpose in this choice."

He stood again, walking to a bookshelf and pulling out a volume of the Ramayana. Opening it to a passage where Lord Rama speaks to Sita about duty and honour, he read aloud, finding strength in the ancient words. "Rama, despite his deep love for Sita, accepted their separation for the greater good. His actions were driven by duty and a profound sense of responsibility. I draw inspiration from his example. My love for Sujata is eternal, but my duty to society and to the principles we both uphold must take precedence."

Mahesh closed the book gently and placed it back on the shelf. "This decision, though it brings personal sorrow, is a testament to the strength of our love and our shared values. In renouncing the idea of marriage, I am not renouncing my love for Sujata; rather, I am elevating it to a higher plane, where it fuels my dedication to our shared goals."

He walked back to the window, the evening now giving way to the night. The stars began to twinkle, each one a reminder of the vastness and mystery of the universe. "In the silence of the night, I find solace. Our love is like these stars, constant and unwavering, even if separated by the vast expanse of the sky. It guides me, inspires me, and gives me strength."

Mahesh took a deep breath, feeling a profound sense of peace. "Sujata, my commitment to you is unwavering. Though we may not share a home or a life in the traditional sense, we share something far more significant – a bond of spirit and purpose. I will continue to support you, not as a husband, but as a comrade, a fellow traveller on this path of service and justice."

He closed his eyes, offering a silent prayer to the universe. "May our choices bring about the change we envision. May our dedication inspire others to rise above personal desires and strive for the greater good. And may our love, though unconventional, remain a beacon of hope and strength for us both."

With these thoughts, Mahesh felt a deep sense of resolution. His path was clear, his purpose renewed. He would continue to work tirelessly for the betterment of society, carrying with him the strength and inspiration drawn from his love for Sujata. Their bond, transcending the constraints of traditional relationships, would forever be a source of motivation and guidance.

As the night deepened, Mahesh returned to his desk, ready to immerse himself in his work once more. The solitude that had once seemed daunting now felt like a sacred space, a testament to the purity and strength of his commitment. He would honour his love for Sujata by dedicating himself to the principles they both cherished, finding fulfilment in the knowledge that their shared mission was greater than any personal desire.

Thus, Mahesh embraced his path with grace and determination, his heart filled with a serene resolve. His love for Sujata, though unfulfilled in the conventional sense, remained a guiding light, illuminating the way forward and inspiring him to continue striving for the greater good.

In the heart of the village, the ancient Puttalli Gacch tree stood as a silent witness to the lives and loves of its people. It had seen generations come and go, their stories etched in its gnarled bark and whispered through its rustling leaves. When news of Sujata and Mahesh's decision to remain apart despite their deep love for each other reached the village, the old tree seemed to shudder with the collective sigh of the community.

The villagers gathered beneath its sprawling branches, seeking solace and understanding in its enduring presence. Among them were elders who had known Sujata as Inara Wali, young ones who idolized Mahesh, and peers who had seen their journey from the beginning. Their voices rose in a murmur of concern and confusion, a chorus of sentiments that echoed the tree's silent lament.

One of the elders, a wise woman named Nirmala, stepped forward to speak. Her voice, though soft, carried the weight of many years and many stories. "We stand here today, beneath this sacred tree, to seek clarity and perhaps, to challenge the decisions made by two of our brightest stars, Sujata and Mahesh. Their separation, though grounded in noble intentions, leaves a void that resonates deeply within our community."

A young man, eager and idealistic, added his voice to the discussion. "Mahesh and Sujata have always been our role models. Their love was an aspiration, a symbol of unity and strength. How can their separation serve the greater good when it leaves behind a trail of sadness and incompleteness?"

Nirmala nodded, her eyes reflecting the pain of the young man. "True, their love has inspired many. Yet, in their decision to remain apart, they invoke the teachings of the Bhagavad Gita and the Upanishads, emphasizing duty and selflessness over personal desires. But we must ask ourselves, can duty and love not coexist? Can their union not strengthen their resolve and bring even greater change to our society?"

An elder named Harish, known for his deep understanding of scriptures and philosophy, stepped forward. "In the Ramayana, Lord Rama and Sita faced separation for the greater good, but their love remained steadfast, a source of strength. Similarly, the Mahabharata teaches us that personal sacrifices are sometimes necessary for the greater cause. Yet, these stories also show that love and duty are not mutually exclusive. They can, and often do, fuel each other."

A young woman, her eyes filled with tears, spoke next. "Sujata has broken barriers and set new standards for us. Her strength is undeniable. But, would her union with Mahesh not symbolize a new kind of partnership, one where love and duty walk hand in hand? Their marriage could be a powerful statement against the traditional constraints that bind us."

The tree seemed to whisper in agreement as a gentle breeze rustled its leaves. The villagers felt a collective shiver, as if the spirit of the Puttalli Gacch was urging them to speak from their hearts.

An older man named Ram Bishwash, who had seen the hardships of life and the beauty of love, stepped into the circle. "Our society has evolved, but remnants of old prejudices and fears remain. Mahesh and Sujata's union could shatter those remnants, showing that love transcends societal expectations and can exist alongside duty. By choosing to remain apart, they may inadvertently strengthen the very barriers they seek to dismantle."

A middle-aged woman, Saraswati, known for her wisdom and practical approach to life, added her voice. "Sujata and Mahesh are symbols of progress and modernity. Their decision to stay apart, though noble, feels like a step back into the shadows of tradition. We need their love to shine brightly, to show us that change does not require the sacrifice of personal happiness."

The villagers nodded; their hearts heavy but their resolve firm. The Puttalli Gacch seemed to pulse with the energy of their collective will, urging them to challenge the separation of two souls meant to be together.

Nirmala, her voice filled with a renewed strength, addressed the gathering once more. "We must reach out to Sujata and Mahesh, not in defiance of their decisions, but in support of a new path. A path where love and duty are not seen as opposing forces, but as complementary ones. Our ancient philosophies teach us balance, and it is this balance that we must advocate for."

As the villagers dispersed, their minds were filled with thoughts of reconciliation and unity. The Puttalli Gacch stood tall and silent, a guardian of their hopes and dreams. They knew that their journey to bring Sujata and Mahesh together would be fraught with challenges, but it was a journey with undertakings in vain.

In the days that followed, the community rallied around their leaders, urging them to reconsider their decision. Letters were written, meetings were held, and prayers were offered. The collective voice of the village, inspired by the ancient tree and guided by the wisdom of their ancestors, sought to bridge the gap between love and duty.

Sujata, upon hearing the heartfelt pleas of their people, found herself deeply moved. But she did not change her decisions.

31

Family Reunion

Time moved on, and with it, the life of Inara Wali i.e. Madam Sujata, the Chief District Officer (CDO), saw significant consolidation. Sujata had not only carved out a prominent career for herself but had also created a sanctuary for her family. Her parents, Rudra and Kushum, along with her parents-in-law, all resided together in the official bungalow provided to her. This residence, equipped with all modern amenities, was a stark contrast to the simpler homes they had known.

Her parents and in-laws found themselves in an unfamiliar world of luxury and comfort. The house boasted contemporary facilities—air conditioning, hot water on demand, a fully equipped kitchen, and plush furnishings. Initially, they were overwhelmed, unsure of how to navigate this new environment. They fumbled with remote controls, marvelled at the microwave's speed, and cautiously enjoyed the comforts of hot showers. Sujata, ever the dutiful daughter, took it upon herself to gently guide them through this transition, ensuring they felt at ease in their new surroundings.

One evening, as the sun dipped below the horizon and cast a warm glow through the large windows, Sujata sat down with her parents in the spacious living room. The aroma of freshly brewed tea wafted through the air, mingling with the comforting scent of home-cooked food.

"Amma, Baba, how are you settling in?" Sujata asked, her voice filled with genuine concern.

Rudra, her father, looked around the room, his eyes lingering on the modern art adorning the walls. "It's all so different, Beti. This house, these gadgets... I feel like we're living in a different world."

Kushum nodded in agreement, her hands resting on her lap. "Yes, Sujata. We never imagined such comfort. It's overwhelming at times."

Sujata smiled, reaching out to hold her mother's hand. "I know it's a big change, but you deserve all this and more. You've worked so hard all your lives, it's time you enjoy the fruits of your labour."

"But Beti," Rudra hesitated, "we don't want to become too accustomed to this. What if we forget where we came from?"

Sujata's eyes softened. "Baba, it's not about forgetting our roots. It's about evolving while cherishing our past. You've taught me humility and hard work. Those lessons are etched in my soul. This new life doesn't erase our history; it builds upon it."

Kushum's eyes moistened with pride. "You've grown into such a wise woman, Sujata. Sometimes, we wonder how we were blessed with a daughter like you."

Sujata chuckled, a playful glint in her eyes. "Well, you did raise me, didn't you? All that wisdom had to come from somewhere."

They laughed together, the sound echoing warmly in the room. These moments of connection, amidst the trappings of their new life, grounded them in their shared history and love.

Days turned into weeks, and the family adapted to their new lifestyle. They no longer hesitated to use the microwave or marvel at the instant hot water. They began to appreciate the conveniences without losing their sense of self. Rudra found joy in tending to the small garden at the back of the house, while Kushum discovered a love for experimenting with new recipes in the well-equipped kitchen.

Sujata ensured that their life was not just about material comforts. She organized regular family gatherings where stories of their past were recounted, and traditional values were reinforced. She invited neighbours and colleagues over, fostering a sense of community and belonging. Her parents and in-laws were treated with respect and reverence by all who visited, which filled them with a sense of pride and dignity.

One afternoon, Sujata and her mother sat on the veranda, enjoying the gentle breeze.

"Amma, do you remember how we used to sit under the neem tree back in Inara Wali, talking for hours?" Sujata reminisced.

Kushum smiled wistfully. "Of course, Beti. Those were simpler times. We had little, but we were content."

"We're still the same people, Amma," Sujata said softly. "Just with different surroundings. Our values, our bond—that's what truly matters."

Kushum placed her hand on Sujata's. "You've given us so much, Sujata. Not just comfort, but respect and love. We're proud of you."

Sujata's eyes filled with tears. "And I'm proud of you, Amma. Everything I am is because of you and Baba."

As the days passed, the house became a true home, filled with love, laughter, and a sense of purpose. Sujata's parents and in-laws embraced their new life, participating in community events and contributing in ways they could. They no longer did the jobs once considered lowly; they had found new roles that brought them dignity and fulfilment.

The transformation was profound, not just in their living conditions, but in their self-perception. They held their heads high, secure in the knowledge that they were valued members of society. This newfound confidence had a ripple effect, inspiring others in the community to aspire for better lives without losing their sense of identity.

Reflecting on this journey, Sujata often pondered the philosophical underpinnings of their transformation. She thought of Puttalli Gacch, an ancient concept that spoke to the cyclical nature of life and the interconnectedness of all beings. According to Puttalli Gacch, life was a continuous cycle of growth, decay, and rebirth, and each stage was essential to the whole.

Sujata saw parallels in their own lives. Their past, marked by simplicity and hardship, was not something to be erased but embraced as the foundation of their present success. Their new life, with all its comforts, was a rebirth that honoured their history while opening doors to future possibilities.

She understood that true progress was not merely about material gain but about evolving in spirit and consciousness. It was about finding balance—acknowledging the past, living fully in the present, and paving the way for a brighter future.

In the quiet moments, Sujata often sat in her garden, contemplating these thoughts. She felt a profound sense of gratitude for the journey that had brought them here. It was not just a journey of physical relocation but of inner transformation—a journey from scarcity to abundance, from anonymity to respect, and from isolation to community.

Sujata knew that their story was just one thread in the vast tapestry of life, but it was a thread woven with resilience, love, and the timeless wisdom of Puttalli Gacch. As she looked at her family, flourishing in their new roles and environment, she felt a deep sense of fulfilment. They were living proof that it was possible to transcend limitations, honour one's roots, and yet, reach for the stars.

And in this harmonious balance, Sujata found her peace, knowing that they had not just changed their destiny but had also set a precedent for generations to come—a legacy of love, respect, and enduring hope.

The Puttalli Gacch, an ancient and venerable tree, had stood for centuries, witnessing the passage of time and the lives of countless villagers. Its broad, gnarled branches provided shade and solace, its roots delved deep into the earth, intertwining with the very soul of the land. It was beneath this majestic tree that Sujata's husband was laid to rest, a place of reverence and peace.

After his death, Sujata found herself drawn to the Puttalli Gacch with an almost magnetic pull. She visited his grave often, offering her respects, her heart heavy with both grief and gratitude for the time they had shared. Sitting beneath the tree, she found a quiet sanctuary where she could connect with her inner self and the memories of her late husband. The tree's presence, ancient and wise, offered her a sense of comfort and continuity.

One warm afternoon, as Sujata sat under the Puttalli Gacch, her mother, Kushum, approached her with gentle steps. She had noticed Sujata's frequent visits and the hours she spent in silent contemplation under the tree. Concerned and curious, she decided to speak with her daughter.

"Sujata, may I join you?" Kushum asked softly, her voice blending with the rustle of the leaves above.

Sujata looked up and smiled, patting the ground beside her. "Of course, Amma. Please, sit."

As Kushum settled down, she gazed at her daughter, noting the serene expression on her face. "I've noticed you come here often, Beti. You spend hours under this tree. What draws you here?"

Sujata took a deep breath, her eyes fixed on the ancient branches above. "Amma, this tree holds a special place in my heart. It's not just because my husband is buried here, though that's part of it. The Puttalli Gacch has stood here for centuries, a silent witness to our lives. It has seen generations come and go, and it offers a connection to the past that I find deeply comforting."

Kushum nodded, understanding the significance of the tree but also harbouring another concern. "I understand, Beti. This tree is indeed special. But I also worry about you. You're still young, and you have so much life ahead of you. Have you thought about your future? About remarrying?"

Sujata turned to face her mother, her eyes clear and resolute. "Amma, I have thought about it. But right now, I find peace and strength in my memories and in my work. This tree, the Puttalli Gacch, reminds me of the enduring nature of life. It stands tall and strong, no matter the storms it faces. I draw strength from that."

Kushum reached out and took Sujata's hand. "I see how much this place means to you, Sujata. But I also want to see you happy. I want to see you find love and companionship again."

Sujata squeezed her mother's hand gently. "I know, Amma. And maybe one day I will. But for now, I'm focusing on my work and the changes we're bringing to our village. This tree... it's a symbol of resilience for me. It reminds me that even in loss, there is strength to be found."

The Puttalli Gacch had indeed been a pillar of the community for as long as anyone could remember. Stories passed down through generations spoke of its origins. It was said that the tree was planted by the village's founder, a wise sage who understood the importance of having a living monument to anchor the community. Over the centuries, the tree grew, its branches spreading wide, offering shade and comfort to all who sought refuge under its canopy.

During times of celebration, the villagers would gather around the Puttalli Gacch. Marriages were blessed beneath its boughs, and festivals were celebrated with its silent blessings. It stood as a witness to the cycles of life, a constant amidst change. Its roots, deep and strong, symbolized the interconnectedness of the villagers and their shared heritage.

For Sujata, the Puttalli Gacch was more than just a tree. It was a spiritual anchor, a place where she felt a profound connection to her past, her heritage, and her late husband. Sitting under its sprawling branches, she often reflected on the lessons of resilience and endurance the tree embodied. It had weathered countless storms, yet it remained standing, strong and persistent. This resilience mirrored her own journey through grief and her determination to continue her work as CDO, bringing positive change to her community.

Sujata's connection to the tree was not merely emotional but philosophical. She saw in it a reflection of the principles she cherished—endurance, strength, and continuity. It reminded her that while life was transient, certain values and connections transcended time. Her visits to the Puttalli Gacch became a meditative practice, a way to align herself with the deeper rhythms of life.

One evening, as the sun set, casting a golden hue over the landscape, Sujata and her mother sat quietly under the tree. The air was filled with the chirping of crickets and the rustle of leaves.

"Amma, do you know the story of how this tree came to be?" Sujata asked, her voice filled with reverence.

Kushum smiled, nodding. "Yes, my mother told me. It was planted by our village's founder, a sage who understood the importance of roots and continuity."

Sujata nodded, a thoughtful expression on her face. "Exactly. This tree has seen everything—births, deaths, celebrations, and tragedies. It stands as a testament to the strength of our community. When I sit here, I feel connected to all those who came before us. It gives me perspective and strength."

Kushum looked at her daughter, pride and love shining in her eyes. "You have always been wise beyond your years, Sujata. Your understanding of life and its complexities is remarkable."

Sujata smiled gently. "Thank you, Amma. This tree reminds me that even in the face of loss, we can find strength and purpose. My work as CDO is my way of honouring the past while building a better future. This tree, the Puttalli Gacch, stands as a reminder that we are all part of a larger whole, and our actions today will shape the future."

As Sujata and her mother sat in silence, enveloped by the ancient presence of the Puttalli Gacch, they reflected on the continuity of life. The tree's existence spanned centuries, a silent observer of the village's history and a symbol of resilience and enduring strength. For Sujata, it was a place of solace and contemplation, a reminder of the interconnectedness of all things.

The philosophy of the Puttalli Gacch was simple yet profound. It taught that life, with all its joys and sorrows, was a cycle of growth and renewal. The tree's roots reached deep into the earth, drawing sustenance and stability, while its branches reached towards the sky, symbolizing aspiration and hope. This balance between grounding and striving was a lesson Sujata embraced fully.

Her frequent visits to the tree were not just acts of mourning but of celebration and renewal. She honoured her late husband's memory while finding the strength to move forward. The tree's shade offered a sanctuary where she could reflect on her purpose and draw inspiration for her work.

Sujata's connection to the Puttalli Gacch also influenced her leadership style. As CDO, she approached her role with the same principles of resilience, continuity, and growth. She worked tirelessly to uplift her community, ensuring that the changes they implemented were sustainable and rooted in the village's traditions and values.

In her heart, Sujata carried the philosophy of the Puttalli Gacch—an enduring belief in the cyclical nature of life and the importance of roots and connections. This belief guided her actions and decisions, shaping her into a compassionate and visionary leader.

Reflecting on the past and looking towards the future, Sujata felt a deep sense of peace. The Puttalli Gacch, with its centuries-old wisdom, had taught her invaluable lessons about life and resilience. It stood as a testament to the enduring spirit of her community, a symbol of strength and continuity.

As the evening shadows lengthened, Sujata and her mother rose, feeling the gentle embrace of the tree's ancient presence. They walked back to their home, hand in hand, their hearts filled with gratitude and hope. The Puttalli Gacch, steadfast and eternal, remained a guiding light, its philosophy deeply woven into the fabric of their lives.

In the quiet moments, Sujata knew that she was not alone. The tree's roots, deeply embedded in the earth, mirrored her own connection to her past and her community. Its branches, reaching towards the heavens, symbolized her aspirations for the future. This balance, this harmony, was the essence of the Puttalli Gacch's wisdom—a wisdom that Sujata carried with her, guiding her on her journey of life, love, and leadership.

32

Bhola Singh's Conspiracy

In the seclusion of their border hideout, Bhola Singh and his three trusted accomplices—Tejas, Munna, and Sudhir—sat in a tight circle, a flickering oil lamp casting eerie shadows on their hardened faces. The night was still, save for the occasional rustle of leaves and the distant cry of nocturnal creatures. It was in this uneasy silence that Bhola Singh unfurled his latest, most sinister plot.

Bhola began, his voice a low, venomous hiss. "We cannot let them forget us. We cannot let them think they have won. We will strike fear into their hearts, make them realize that without our presence, chaos reigns."

Tejas leaned forward, his eyes glinting with malicious intent. "What do you propose, Bhola? We've been in hiding long enough. It's time for action."

Bhola's lips curled into a cruel smile. "We will target their very livelihood. We will burn their thatched houses, steal their cattle, and poison their wells. Let them taste despair. They will come running back to the affluents, begging for protection."

Munna, ever the brute, thumped his fist on the ground. "Burning houses and stealing cattle—this will cripple them. They rely on their livestock for everything. If we take that away, they will be broken."

Sudhir, the cold strategist, added, "And destroying their water sources will ensure their desperation. They will have no choice but to depend on the affluent families for survival. It's a ruthless plan, but it will work."

Their grim consensus reached; the men began to lay out the details. Tejas would lead the arson attacks, selecting the most vulnerable thatched houses in each village. Munna, with his strength and stealth, would steal the cattle in the dead of night, leading them deep into the forest where they would be abandoned. Sudhir, with his knowledge of herbs and poisons, would contaminate the village wells, ensuring that the very essence of life became a source of fear and disease.

Over the next few weeks, the plot unfolded with ruthless precision. One by one, the villages were struck under the cover of darkness. The flames of burning thatched houses illuminated the night sky, casting a haunting glow that could be seen from miles away. Families awoke to the horror of their homes engulfed in fire, the acrid smell of smoke filling their lungs. Cattle, their lifeblood, disappeared without a trace, their cries echoing through the forests before being swallowed by the darkness. Wells, once sources of refreshment, turned into harbingers of illness, their waters tainted and undrinkable.

Panic spread like wildfire among the villagers. Fear took root in their hearts as they saw their livelihoods destroyed systematically. The affluent families, untouched by the chaos, watched from a distance, their power and influence seemingly unassailable. The once proud and independent villagers now found themselves teetering on the brink of despair, their sense of security shattered.

Madam Sujata, ever vigilant and resilient, quickly recognized the pattern of destruction. Gathering the village leaders, she addressed them with a stern resolve. "This is not mere coincidence. These attacks are coordinated. We must stand together and protect our communities. We will not succumb to fear."

Superintendent Shri Mohan Lal, informed of the escalating crisis, mobilized his forces. Patrols were increased, and checkpoints were established around the villages. Investigations were launched to trace the origins of the attacks, and informants were placed in strategic locations to gather intelligence on Bhola Singh and his gang.

Madam Sujata, undeterred by the threats to her own life, led from the front. She organized community meetings, urging the villagers to remain vigilant and united. Water sources were closely monitored, and alternative supplies were arranged to prevent a health crisis. Volunteers were trained in fire prevention and response, and night watches were established to guard against further cattle thefts.

Despite these efforts, the fear persisted. The villagers, once self-reliant and confident, were now haunted by the spectre of further attacks. Rumours spread like the wind; each story more terrifying than the last. The affluent families, sensing an opportunity, began to extend offers of protection, demanding loyalty and subservience in return.

Madam Sujata, aware of the delicate balance, intensified her efforts. She personally visited each affected village, bringing supplies and moral support. Her presence, reassured many, but the underlying fear remained.

The police, under Superintendent Lal's directive, combed the forests and questioned suspects, slowly closing in on Bhola Singh's hideout. The criminal mastermind, however, remained elusive, his cunning and knowledge of the terrain allowing him to stay one step ahead.

In a clandestine meeting, Superintendent Lal and Madam Sujata discussed the next steps. "We need to cut off their supply lines and disrupt their operations," Lal stated. "Bhola Singh thrives on fear and chaos. If we remove his ability to cause harm, we will neutralize him."

Sujata nodded in agreement. "We must also strengthen the community's resilience. Fear is his greatest weapon, and unity is ours. We will continue to support the villagers, ensuring they do not fall back into the dependency on the affluent families."

As the days turned into weeks, a relentless pursuit ensued. The police, aided by informants and local trackers, began to close the net around Bhola Singh and his gang. Skirmishes in the dense forests became more frequent, each encounter bringing the law enforcement closer to their elusive quarry.

Finally, a breakthrough occurred. An informant provided crucial intelligence about Bhola Singh's hideout deep within the forest. Superintendent Lal, leading a specialized task force, launched a swift and decisive operation. The confrontation was intense, but Bhola

Singh and his men, realizing their time was up, attempted a desperate escape.

The ensuing chase was fraught with peril. Bhola Singh, Tejas, Munna, and Sudhir, using their intimate knowledge of the terrain, led the police on a gruelling pursuit through the thick underbrush and rugged hills. The task force, driven by determination and guided by the informant's insights, slowly closed the gap.

Cornered near a ravine, Bhola Singh and his men made a final stand. The air was thick with tension as the law enforcement officers, armed and resolute, surrounded them. In a last-ditch effort, Bhola Singh attempted to negotiate, but Superintendent Lal, unwavering in his duty, demanded their immediate surrender.

Seeing no escape, Bhola Singh, his face a mask of defiance and resignation, lowered his weapon. The men were apprehended, their reign of terror finally brought to an end. As they were led away in handcuffs, the villagers, informed of the successful operation, began to breathe a collective sigh of relief.

Madam Sujata, receiving the news, immediately set out to visit the affected villages. Her arrival was met with a mixture of joy and gratitude. She addressed the gathered crowds, her voice filled with compassion and determination. "The threat has been neutralized, but our work is not over. We must rebuild, stronger and more united than before. Together, we will ensure that fear does not dictate our lives."

Under her guidance, the villages began the arduous process of recovery. Houses were rebuilt, cattle were gradually replaced, and water sources were restored to their former purity. The community, galvanized by the ordeal, emerged more resilient and self-reliant.

Superintendent Lal, reflecting on the harrowing weeks, acknowledged the crucial role played by Madam Sujata and the unyielding spirit of the villagers. "It is through unity and perseverance that we overcame this challenge. Let this be a lesson that even in the face of fear and chaos, we can find strength and hope."

The tale of Bhola Singh's plot and its eventual unravelling became a part of the village lore, a stark reminder of the thin line between order and chaos, and the enduring power of community and resilience in the face of adversity.

In the grand tapestry of human existence, the tale of Bhola Singh and his insidious plot to terrorize the villages serves as a stark reminder of the perennial struggle between light and darkness, order and chaos, hope and despair. The villagers, thrust into the throes of uncertainty and fear, found themselves standing at the precipice of ruin, their lives and livelihoods threatened by the machinations of a few. Yet, within this crucible of adversity, a profound truth emerged: the indomitable spirit of humanity, when kindled by unity and resilience, can overcome even the most formidable of challenges.

Philosophers throughout the ages have pondered the nature of evil and its capacity to disrupt the sensitive balance of society. As Socrates once mused, "The greatest way to live with honour in this world is to be what we pretend to be." Bhola Singh and his men, cloaked in the pretence of benevolent authority, sought to instil terror and subjugation, yet their actions revealed a stark dissonance between their true nature and the guise they adopted. It is in this dichotomy that we find the essence of their eventual downfall.

For in the heart of the villagers, despite the flames that razed their homes and the poisoned wells that threatened their survival, there burned a brighter flame—one of solidarity and unwavering resolve. As the German philosopher Friedrich Nietzsche posited, "That which does not kill us makes us stronger." The villagers, though battered by the onslaught, drew strength from their shared suffering, transforming their pain into a collective force of resistance and renewal.

Madam Sujata and Superintendent Lal, embodying the principles of justice and compassion, became the pillars upon which the community rebuilt its shattered foundations. Their actions echoed the timeless wisdom of Confucius: "It does not matter how slowly you go as long as you do not stop." With patience and perseverance, they led the villagers through the darkest of nights, never ceasing in their efforts to restore peace and order. Their leadership was not merely a response to crisis but a reaffirmation of the enduring human capacity for empathy and courage.

In the philosophical discourse, the concept of evil is often juxtaposed with the inherent goodness that resides within the human soul. Augustine of Hippo once wrote, "Since love grows within you, so beauty grows. For love is the beauty of the soul." The heinous acts of Bhola Singh were an attempt to sow discord and hatred, yet in the aftermath, it was the love and solidarity among the villagers that prevailed. The community's response, guided by love and mutual respect, transformed the narrative from one of victimhood to one of empowerment.

The strategic arson, the theft of cattle, and the poisoning of water sources were intended to fracture the community, to render it dependent and pliable to the will of the affluent. However, as Marcus Aurelius aptly stated, "The soul becomes dyed with the colour of its thoughts." The villagers, refusing to succumb to despair, instead infused their collective consciousness with thoughts of hope and resilience. This mental fortitude, coupled with their unwavering spirit, rendered Bhola Singh's scheme ultimately impotent.

Moreover, the incident underscores a deeper philosophical reflection on the nature of power and its ethical implications. The French philosopher Michel Foucault contended that "Power is everywhere... because it comes from everywhere." Bhola Singh's attempt to wield power through fear and coercion was met with the realization that true power lies not in domination, but in the collective will of a united community. The villagers, through their solidarity and mutual support, reclaimed the narrative of power, demonstrating that ethical leadership and communal resilience are the bedrocks of a just society.

In the aftermath of the ordeal, as the villagers rebuilt their homes and reclaimed their lives, they embodied the essence of the ancient Stoic philosophy: "The impediment to action advances action. What stands in the way becomes the way." The very obstacles that Bhola Singh placed before them became the crucible through which their strength and unity were forged. Each act of rebuilding, each gesture of support among neighbours, was a testament to their collective defiance against tyranny and fear.

The tale of Bhola Singh's terror and the villagers' courageous response thus transcends mere narrative; it becomes a philosophical exploration of the human condition. It is a reminder that within each of us lies the potential for both great good and profound evil, and it is the choices we make, individually and collectively, that determine the trajectory of our lives and communities. As the French philosopher Jean-Paul Sartre famously declared, "Man is condemned to be free; because once thrown into the world, he is responsible for everything he does."

Ultimately, the villagers' triumph over adversity reaffirms the enduring human capacity for resilience and hope. It is a poignant reminder that even in the face of the most daunting challenges, the human spirit, guided by love, solidarity, and ethical leadership, can overcome the forces of chaos and fear. In this timeless struggle between light and darkness, it is the light of the human soul, burning ever brighter in the hearts of those who stand united, that prevails.

33

Finale of the Legend

In the small village of Malanga, the cruel grip of cholera ravaged the populace, claiming lives with a remorseless hand. Amongst the chaos and despair, a young boy named Satish found himself forsaken by both family and community, his plight a stark emblem of the harsh realities he faced. Deprived of medicinal aid, he stood alone, a solitary figure resigned to the whims of fate, his path obscured by the shadows of neglect and social turmoil.

Upon hearing of Satish's deteriorating health, Sujata hastened to his side with a heart gripped by tumultuous anguish forgetting her security protocol. Despite her sorrow, her eyes remained dry as the desert sands. The spectre of death loomed ominously close, casting its dark shadow upon the boy. With tender care, she cradled his weary head in her lap, offering him a sanctuary of solace amidst the encroaching darkness. She stood with hands clasped and head veiled, her gaze turned towards the setting sun as she offered up a fervent prayer that seemed to reach beyond the heavens. The hushed reverence of her devotion lingered briefly before the harsh reality intruded.

In the distance, ominous black clouds unfurled, whispering foreboding tales across the sky. Despite her efforts, Satish, struggled to awaken from his slumber, his eyelids heavy with an unseen weight. Desperation clawed at Sujata's heart as she shook him vigorously, her cries lost amidst the impending tempest. Yet, the hand of fate remained unyielding, its decree immutable. In an instant, the radiant hopes she held dear were snuffed out, consumed by the raging storm that descended upon his world, leaving nothing but echoes of sorrow in its wake.

In her moment of need, an unknown man named Bhanu Singh emerged. Yet, his stride lacked its usual vigour; it seemed fractured, as if burdened by unseen weights. His countenance betrayed the turmoil within, his eyes ablaze with an inferno of unchecked rage. From the depths of his pocket, he withdrew a gleaming penknife, a symbol of his faltering masculinity, and with deliberate strokes, he trimmed his moustache in a futile attempt to bolster his fading strength. With a savage grip, he seized Sujata by her tresses, dragging her mercilessly towards the shadows of Puttali Gacch. There, he enacted a grotesque symphony of violence, rending her flesh at countless junctures, heedless to her anguished cries for aid—a solitary echo in the desolate night. As crimson streams painted the earth beneath her, she found an unexpected ally in the embrace of Puttali Gacch, whose leafy canopy sought to soothe her wounds, tenderly imparting a maternal affection unknown to her until that moment. Meanwhile, Inara Wali, the silent witness to this macabre ballet, remained stoically impassive, refusing to exhale a single breath anew, as if acknowledging the inevitable descent into darkness.

Amidst the convergence of souls from distant realms and nearby lands, none could breach the earth to grant Sujata a resting place. The soil, once yielding, now held fast, a fortress against intrusion. Not even a whisper of wind dared disturb the stillness that enshrouded the scene. A hush, profound and reverent, embraced the space. Yet, in a spectacle that defied explanation, the form of Inara Wali eluded their searching gazes. With furrowed brows and hearts heavy with disbelief, they cast their eyes left and right, only to find emptiness—a vacancy profound and unsettling

During those fateful hours, ambulances and district authorities arrived. Bhanu Singh was shot dead. It was discovered that Bhanu Singh was the brother-in-law of Bhola Singh. Inara Wali, now known as Sujata, lay on a hospital bed. It took her months to recover. Villagers from far and wide offered prayers for her speedy recovery. Finally, a month later, she stood as usual, strong and firm.

Since that fateful moment, the boughs of Puttali Gacch bore no verdant burden. Bereft, it stood yet resilient, defying the ravages of time and circumstance. Through epochs and epochs hence, it has stood resolute, a testament to the enduring spirit that courses through its gnarled veins. Neither the passing of Mahesh nor the fading of Sujata could dim its grandeur, for Puttali Gacch endures, steadfast in its place, as if ordained to traverse boundless horizons, with miles yet to tread and miles and miles beyond.

In the saga of social change, Sujata CDO emerges as a guiding light, embodying the essence of education, justice, equal opportunity, and human dignity. Her journey is a transformative power of relentless determination and compassionate leadership. Sujata's advocacy transcends mere action; it is a philosophical statement—a proclamation of the inherent worth and potential of every individual. Her legacy serves as a potent reminder that true progress is not measured by accolades but by the impact we have on the lives of others. Let us heed her call to action, to champion justice, equality, and dignity for all. In honouring Sujata, we honour the very essence of humanity's highest ideals.

The Legend of Inara Wali carried on with untold stories of her success and resilience. Her legacy became intertwined with the ancient tree, both symbols of survival and strength in the face of overwhelming adversity. And so, the tale of Sujata and Puttali Gacch was etched into the annals of history, a striking end note to a story of profound sorrow, unyielding courage, and enduring hope, indeed!!!

www.ingramcontent.com/pod-product-compliance
Lightning Source LLC
LaVergne TN
LVHW091625070526
838199LV00044B/944